African American Pamphlet Collection, Henry Jarvis Raymond

Disunion And Slavery

In a Series of Letters

African American Pamphlet Collection, Henry Jarvis Raymond

Disunion And Slavery
In a Series of Letters

ISBN/EAN: 9783744732109

Printed in Europe, USA, Canada, Australia, Japan

Cover: Foto ©ninafisch / pixelio.de

More available books at **www.hansebooks.com**

DISUNION AND SLAVERY.

A SERIES OF LETTERS

TO

Hon. W. L. YANCEY, of Alabama,

· BY

HENRY J. RAYMOND, of New York.

I.

THE NORTHERN STATES AND THE SLAVE TRADE IN 1787.

NEW-YORK, Nov. 23, 1860.

Hon. W. L. YANCEY—Sir : I have read your reply of Nov. 9 to an editorial article in the TIMES of Oct. 27, in which you claim to have corrected what you style the " hostile and malignant criticisms of two leading editors in the Black Republican cause, viz.: Mr. THURLOW WEED and Mr. HENRY J. RAYMOND,"—upon your speeches in the North during the recent Presidential canvass. As you have thus given the matter a personal direction, you will excuse me for giving you a personal answer.

Let me say, in the first place, that you have no right to characterize those criticisms as either "hostile or malignant." They are perfectly fair and legitimate comments upon public speeches on public topics. Of all men, you should be the last to reproach your political opponents at the North with discourtesy. You spoke in nearly all our principal cities, to large audiences, two-thirds of whom had not the slightest sympathy with your views, or the least respect for the object you sought to accomplish. But you were heard with the most respectful attention. In no instance was there the slightest indication of personal disrespect ;—in no case were you interrupted, or even questioned on any point. You were heard everywhere with just as much deference and courtesy, as if every word you uttered had accorded fully with the opinions and sentiments of those you addressed. If you will contrast this reception with that which would have greeted any one of your opponents, who should attempt to address the people of your own section on the same subject, you will find no ground for claiming superiority over us in the matter of courtesy.

The object of your visit to the North was to vindicate the claim put forth by Southern politicians, of the right to increase and extend the institution of Slavery. You attempted this, in your speeches, first by showing, as a matter of history, that the framers of the Constitution regarded the increase of Slavery as desirable for the country, and made specific provision for it in the Constitution itself ; and, secondly, by showing, as a matter of statistics, that Slavery is a benefit to the States in which it exists, and to the North through its trade with those States. Under the first head you asserted that Massachusets "took the lead," in the Convention that framed the Constitution, in "insisting" that the Slave-trade should not be prohibited until 1808, and afterwards in placing this clause beyond the reach of amendment. I have characterized this assertion as a perversion of the facts of history ;—and your letter of Nov. 9 is an attempt to vindicate your assertion against this criticism. It is not enough for you to show that Massachusetts assented to these measures. No one disputes or doubts that fact,—nor did we need a missionary from Alabama to inform us of it. Your assertion was much broader, and its object was very different. You represented that Massachusetts, as the head of the Northern Colonies. "insisted" on continuing the Slave-trade for twenty years longer, for the specific purpose of " widening the basis of Slavery," and " increasing the number of slaves,"—while Virginia, as the head of the Southern Colonies, resisted the attempt. And you made this representation for the purpose of basing upon it the appeal to the people of the North, that, as their fathers had thus clearly declared their approval of Slavery, and provided for its increase,—and had forced this increase upon the South,—it was unjust for them, their descendants, to denounce and restrict it now.

Now, I did say that this line of argument showed that you were either very imperfectly informed in the history of the country, or very reckless and unscrupulous in the statement of facts. The first horn of the dilemma I abandon. Your quotations from the Madison Papers,—and the sagacious manner in which you have weeded out from the passages relating to this question everything which makes against your position, shows that you are not "imperfectly informed" on this subject. Nor is it quite fair to say that you are "reckless and unscrupulous" in your statements. Those moods imply a certain degree of indifference as to the truth or falsehood of statements made; while you are exceedingly careful, first to make a statement which is exactly the opposite of the truth, and then to make it plausible by scrupulously falsifying the public records by which it is to be tested. That I have full warrant for this serious charge, I shall prove by appending to this letter the full debate on that clause of the Constitution which relates to the prohibition of the Slave-trade, on which you base your statement, and from which you have pretended in your letter to quote evidence of its truth. You accuse me of having given "garbled extracts" from that debate. In order to show at whose door that charge justly lies, I copy your letter, including the debate as you have professed to quote it.

Now, you will see from this record, what you very well knew before, that neither Massachusetts, nor any other Northern State, "insisted" that the Slave-trade should not be prohibited by Congress until 1808; that on the contrary, they demanded that the General Government should have power to prohibit it at once; and that they yielded their consent to its continuance for twenty years, only to threats of secession on the part of South Carolina and Georgia, and for the purpose of securing the adhesion of those States to the Union. Mr. PINCKNEY in that debate declared, "South Carolina can never receive the plan if it prohibits the Slave-trade." Gen. PINCKNEY said he "should consider the re-action of the clause as an exclusion of South Carolina from the Union." Mr. BALDWIN, of Georgia, said, "Georgia was decided on this point," and that "it might be understood in what light she would view an attempt to abridge one of her favorite prerogatives." Mr. WILLIAMSON, of North Carolina, "thought the Southern States could not be members of the Union if the clause should be rejected." Mr. RUTLEDGE said, "if the Convention thinks that North Carolina, South Carolina and Georgia will ever agree to the plan, unless their right to import slaves be untouched, the expectation is vain." These quotations are all from the debate on this proposition. These delararations were made by leading Southern men, and were the turning points of the action of the Convention upon that clause. Yet, you have not quoted a single one of them in your citations from that debate. Why not? Because they would have rendered it impossible for you to attribute this action of the Convention, and of the Northern States, to the motive you had assigned—namely, a desire to continue the Slave-trade, in order to "increase the number of slaves," and widen "the basis of Slavery." If you had quoted them, they would have furnished the explanation of the sentences you quote from New-England men. They would have shown that not a single man from Massachusetts, or any other Northern colony, said one solitary syllable in favor of Slavery or of continuing the Slave-trade;—and that their only motive for assenting to it at all was the fear that without such assent the formation of the Union would be impossible. And to induce them still further to yield their hostility to it, the Southern delegation held out hopes that, if the matter were left open, the Southern States themselves might prohibit the traffic. Mr. PINCKNEY said, "If the Southern States are left alone, they will probably of themselves stop importations:"—and again, "If the States be left at liberty on this subject, South Carolina may, perhaps, by degrees do, of herself, what is wished, as Virginia and Maryland have already done." Mr. BALDWIN said of Georgia,—"If left to herself she may probably put a stop to the evil." It was by such alternate threats and promises that the Northern delegates were induced to assent to the compromise proposed by the Committee to which the subject was recommitted,—namely that the trade should not be prohibited before 1800,—and also to the amendment offered by Mr. PINCKNEY, of South Carolina, making it 1808.

It is impossible to suppose that you were ignorant of these facts,—or that you could possibly have mistaken the motive of this action of the Northern delegates.

You quote from RUFUS KING the remark that "the subject should be considered in a political light only," and draw the inference that he and his State, as well as Connecticut, were indifferent to its moral aspects, which Virginia urged so warmly. You say:

"The prohibition was warmly supported on moral grounds by Virginia,—and Connecticut immediately pronounced, 'Let every State import what it pleases.'—while Massachusetts ably seconded Connecticut that it was 'to be considered in a political light only.'"

This is a very adroit arrangement of words, true in themselves, but so arranged as to convey a very gross and palpable falsehood. You represent Connecticut as following the moral protest of Virginia by the exclamation, "let every State import what it pleases," as if protesting against that moral view of the case,—whereas Mr. ELLSWORTH used those words after Mr. RUTLEDGE, of South Carolina, had declared that "religion and humanity had nothing to do with this question," and that "the true question is whether the Southern States shall or shall not be parties to the Union ;—and he added, as a salvo to his own mind, "the morality or wisdom of Slavery are considerations belonging to the States themselves." Mr. KING's remark was not made until the next day, and then related to what had been said of the refusal of South Carolina and Georgia to join the Union, instead of anything that had been said on behalf of Connecticut. If you had any desire to submit Mr. KING's sentiments on this whole subject, why did you not quote what he said upon it on the 8th of August, when the question of representation was under debate.

"Mr. KING had hoped that some accommodation would have taken place on this subject; that at least a time would have been limited for the importation of slaves. *He never could agree to let them be imported without limitation,* and then be represented in the National Legislature. *Indeed, he would so little persuade himself of the rectitude of such a practice, that he was not sure he could assent to it under any circumstances.*" [*Madison Papers, III.,* 1,262.]

You quote Gov. MORRIS, of Pennsylvania, as proposing to recommit the clause for the purpose of making a bargain between the North and South —and sneeringly say it was made a "subject of *trade,* and not of moral speculation." Let me commend to any to whom you may have given such an impression of his views, the following speech made by him on the same subject and on the same occasion:

From the *Madison Papers, Vol. III., page* 1,263.

Mr. GOUVERNEUR MORRIS moved to insert "free" before the word "inhabitants." Much, he said, would depend on this point. *He never would concur in upholding domestic Slavery.* It was a nefarious institution. It was the curse of Heaven on the States where it prevailed. Compare the free regions of the Middle States, where a rich and noble cultivation marks the prosperity and happiness of the people, with the misery and poverty which overspread the barren waste of Virginia, Maryland, and the other States having slaves. Travel through the whole continent, and you behold the prospect continually varying with the appearance and disappearance of Slavery. The moment you leave the Eastern States, and enter New-York, the effects of the institution become visible. Passing through the Jerseys and entering Pennsylvania, every criterion of superior improvement witnesses the change. Proceed southwardly, and every step you take, through the great regions of slaves, presents a desert increasing with the increasing proportion of these wretched beings. Upon what principle is it that the slaves shall be computed in the representation? Are they men? Then make them citizens and let them vote. Are they property? Why, then, is no other property included? The houses in this city (Philadelphia) are worth more than all the wretched slaves who cover the rice swamps of South Carolina. The admission of slaves into the representation, when fairly explained, comes to this: that the inhabitant of Georgia and South Carolina who goes to the Coast of Africa, and in defiance of the most sacred laws of humanity, tears away his fellow-creatures from their dearest connections, and damns them to a most cruel bondage, shall have more votes in a government instituted for protection of the rights of mankind than the citizen of Pennsylvania or New-Jersey, *who views with a laudable horror so nefarious a practice.* He would add that domestic Slavery is the most prominent feature in the aristocratic countenance of the proposed Constitution. The vassalage of the poor has ever been the favorite offspring of aristocracy. And what is the proposed compensation to the Northern States for a sacrifice of every principle of right, of every impulse of humanity? They are to bind themselves to march their militia for the defence of the Southern States, for their defence against these very slaves of whom they complain. They must supply vessels and seamen in case of foreign attack. The Legislature will have indefinite power to tax them by excises and duties on imports, both of which will fall heavier on them than on the Southern inhabitants; for the Bohea tea used by a Northern freeman will pay more tax than the whole consumption of the miserable slave, which consists of nothing more than his physical subsistence and the rag that covers his nakedness. On the other side, the Southern States are not to be restrained from importing fresh supplies of wretched Africans, at once to increase the danger of attack and the difficulty of defence; nay, *they are to be encouraged to it,* by an assurance of having their votes in the National

Government increased in proportion, and are at the same time to have their exports and their slaves exempt from all contributions for the public service. Let it not be said that direct taxation is to be proportioned to representation. It is idle to suppose that the General Government can stretch its hand directly into the pockets of the people, scattered over so vast a country. They can only do it through the medium of exports, imports and excises. For what, then, are all the sacrifices to be made? *He would sooner submit himself to a tax for paying for all the negroes in the United States, than saddle posterity with such a Constitution.*

Does that look like making this a "subject of trade" merely? Does that look like "insisting" on a continuance of the Slave-trade for twenty years?

But I have said quite enough to show the utter falsity of your assertion that Massachusetts, as the head of the Northern Colonies, "*insisted* that the Slave-trade should not be prohibited by Congress until 1808," in order to "increase the number of slaves, and to widen the basis of Slavery." A few words now upon the other branch of this assertion, namely, that it was done against the wish of Virginia, as the representative of the Southern Colonies, and thus forced upon them.

It is true, and is greatly to her honor, that Virginia did resist the continuance of the Slave-trade. She had prohibited that traffic for herself, and urged its prohibition for all the States. But she did not do this as "the head of the Southern Colonies;" she was not acting on their behalf, nor had she their support. On the contrary, she was denounced, and her motives for it assailed then, as they have been since. "As to Virginia," says Gen. PINCKNEY, "she will gain by stopping the importation. Her slaves will rise in value, and she has more than she wants." This is very much in the vein of South Carolina comments upon Virginia now. It is quite in the spirit of your remarks at Montgomery, in 1858, when you advocated the reopening of the Slave-trade, and denounced the "old fogies" of Virginia—JEFFERSON, MADISON and others—who "held opinions on this subject which are not now considered sound."

How the other Southern Colonies regarded the proposition to prohibit the Slave-trade has been made apparent already. Maryland and Virginia had abolished the traffic. Delaware had none to abolish. The only other Southern Colonies were North Carolina, South Carolina and Georgia: and they distinctly refused to join the Union, if Congress were clothed with power to prohibit the Slave-trade. And it was that threat which induced Massachusetts and the other Northern Colonies to assent to the compromise proposed by the Committee.

So much for the manner in which this clause came into the Constitution. If historical records prove anything, they prove that it was inserted on the demand of the principal Southern Colonies, backed by a threat of secession if it were not granted;—and that Massachusetts and the other Northern Colonies conceded it solely and exclusively for the sake of securing the adherence of

4

those Colonies to the Union. Gen. PINCKNEY, in Convention, acknowledged "the liberal conduct" of the Eastern States on this occasion, and was willing to return it by concessions on the subject of commerce. You, on the contrary, attempt to distort it into an indorsement of Slavery and an approval of the Slave-trade. I submit to the public judgment whether you do not thus convict yourself of being utterly "unscrupulous" in the use of historical facts.

Now I might very well stop here, for what I have already said covers the ground of your letter. It settles the question as to the part taken by the Northern and Southern Colonies respectively in regard to the Slave-trade, and the motives by which each section was actuated. But as that was only an incidental point in your speech, permit me to refer to the other branch of your main argument, and the practical policy which it was intended to support.

You have been engaged now for several years in the endeavor to secure the repeal of the laws of Congress prohibiting the Slave-trade, and to restore the full freedom of that traffic to the Southern States. At the South you are seeking to accomplish that result—precisely as South Carolina and Georgia sought the continuance of the trade in the Federal Convention, by menaces of disunion. At the North you held a different language. You asserted that the Fathers of the Republic—the framers of the Constitution—deeming an increase of Slavery desirable, provided for it by keeping the Slave-trade open until 1808. I have shown how utterly baseless—how wanton a perversion of historical fact—that statement is, so far as Massachusetts and the other Northern colonies were concerned. I could prove, by a similar array of equally conclusive testimony, that the statement is just as false, so far as it assigns a motive to the action of the other colonies and to the leading statesmen of the whole country. You, probably, are not ignorant of the fact that on the 20th of October, 1774, the Continental Congress passed a preamble and resolutions solemnly pledging themselves, "under the sacred ties of virtue, honor and love of our country,"

" That we will neither import nor purchase any Slave imported after the first day of December next ;—after which time we will wholly discontinue the Slave-trade, and will neither be concerned in it ourselves, nor will we hire our vessels nor sell our commodities or manufactures to those who are concerned in it."

This was the tone and temper of the people at the outset of our national career. It was the policy which the framers of the Constitution desired to adopt. It was the same sentiment which prompted MASON and MORRIS and RUFUS KING and LUTHER MARTIN to denounce Slavery as a curse to the country, and to insist that the General Government should have power to check its growth by prohibiting its increase and stopping the Slave-trade at once and forever. But it is unnecessary to quote their declarations or enter upon any further historical inquiry on this subject. You have yourself conceded

that the main obstacle which you encounter in your efforts to secure the reopening of the Slave-trade, lies in the fact that the fathers of the Republic were opposed to it. I have before me a copy of the speech made by you in the Southern Commercial Convention, held in Montgomery, May, 1858, on the subject of reopening the African Slave-trade ; and in that speech I find you saying :

" If it were not for the names of MADISON, RANDOLPH, MASON and others, whose names have been quoted in order to frown down the presumption of a young man at this day for pretending to understand this subject, I would even now throw the lance of debate to any gentleman to stand up here and maintain that these laws were constitutional per se. I would to God every countryman of mine was disposed to judge of the issues between the North and South for himself, that the opinions of old fogydom could be utterly wiped out. * * * Will my friend (Mr. PRYOR) now say that Mr. JEFFERSON, in his political ethics on Slavery, was right ? He cannot say so. Mr. JEFFERSON thought it would weaken the South, and, therefore, he was for the entire prohibition of the Slave-trade. The distinguished, venerable, practical and philosophical gentleman from Virginia (Mr. RUFFIN) knows that Mr. Jefferson was wrong in his ideas about Slavery. I need not expatiate on that subject, because it is a matter of history known to everybody. If that was the fact, there was among the framers of the Constitution, who were true to us in all the interests of the white man, a sentiment in relation to Slavery that is not entertained now.

Mr. PRYOR—That is true.

Mr. YANCEY—That is all I ask. Then I say that the old fogies of that day entertained opinions in relation to Slavery, which we of this day are unanimously agreed were not sound. * * * If I could get this body to divest themselves of the shackles that MADISON, JEFFERSON and MASON have thrown about them concerning Slavery, and could get them to understand that South Carolina is against any, even the most limited, prohibition of the Slave-trade, I should not fear their unbiased judgment."

So much for the historical part of the argument by which you endeavored to convince the people of the North that Slavery ought to be increased.

Your next point was to prove by statistics that Slavery is a great blessing to the country, because it had made the South much richer than Free Labor had made the North. And your argument was this :—The wealth of any country is measured by its exports,—that is, by the surplus of its products after its own wants have been supplied out of them. Now the South exports annually of her products to the amount of $200,000,000, while the North exports of hers only a little over $100,000,000. Therefore, the South, which depends upon Slave Labor, is nearly twice as rich as the North, which relies upon Free Labor. Without entering upon any detailed examination of this point, (although the more closely it is examined the more clearly will its sophisty appear,) it is enough to say that the fallacy lies in your skillful manipulation of the word exports. The exports of the North do really and truly measure the surplus products of the North : but the South exports her whole crop. She does not consume any of her cotton at home,—or at least not enough to affect the argument : she exports the whole of it. Yet all the supplies which she draws from the North— her cotton goods, her manufactured woolens, her plantation tools, her teas, silks and imported luxuries, a very large proportion of her bacon, her beef and other provisions—all these are paid for out of the proceeds of her cotton crop,—and generally in advance. She sends that crop to market burdened with the debt incurred for these supplies. Before she can claim that crop as *exports*,—that is, as the *surplus* of her products over her own consumption,—she must deduct that debt. Now you go on to state in these very speeches, that these domestic purchases made at the North, to supply the wants of the Southern States, amount to nearly two hundred millions of dollars every year. Deduct that amount from the exports of the South,—and then see how much you will have left, as the measure of the wealth of the Southern States.

But I shall not extend this letter, likely at best to be much too long, by any further comments upon this point. I send you with it the report of a speech made by me during the canvass, at Rochester, in which I have treated it somewhat more fully.

Leaving this branch of the subject, therefore, I propose to say something of the DISUNION MOVE-MENT now in progress, of which I consider you, to a greater degree than any other man now living, the author and the head. As I desire to treat it somewhat fully,—more so than the limits left me in this communication will permit,—I shall make it the subject of a second letter.

—— 0 ——

The Debate in the Convention of 1787 on the Prohibition of the Slave-Trade.

From the Madison Papers, Vol. III., pp. 1388, et seq.

TUESDAY, Aug. 21.

Mr. L. MARTIN, of Maryland, proposed to vary article 7, section 4, so as to allow a prohibition or tax on the importation of slaves. In the first place, as five slaves are to be counted as three freemen, in the apportionment of Representatives, such a clause would leave an encouragement to this traffic. In the second place, slaves weakened one part of the Union, which the other parts were bound to protect; the privilege of importing them was, therefore, unreasonable. And, in the third place, it was inconsistent with the principles of the Revolution, and dishonorable to the American character, to have such a feature in the Constitution.

Mr. RUTLEDGE, of South Carolina, did not see how the importation of slaves could be encouraged by this section. He was not apprehensive of insurrection, and would readily exempt the other States from the obligation to protect the Southern against them. Religion and humanity had nothing to do with this question. Interest alone is the governing principle with nations. The true question at present is, *whether the Southern States shall or shall not be parties to the Union.* If the Northern States consult their interest, they will not oppose the increase of slaves, which will increase the commodities of which they will become the carriers.

Mr. ELLSWORTH, of Connecticut, was for leaving the clause as it stands. Let every State import what it pleases. The morality or wisdom of Slavery are considerations *belonging to the States themselves*. What enriches a part, enriches the whole, and the States are the best judges of their particular interest. The old Confederation had not meddled with this point, and he did not see any greater necessity for bringing it within the policy of the new one.

Mr. PINCKNEY, of South Carolina—*South Carolina can never receive the plan if it prohibits the Slave-trade.* In every proposed extension of the powers of Congress, that State has expressly and watchfully excepted that of meddling with the importation of negroes. If the States be left at liberty on this subject, South

Carolina may, perhaps, by degrees, do of herself what is wished, as Virginia and Maryland have already done.

Adjourned.

WEDNESDAY, AUG. 22.

In Convention—Article 7, Section 4, was resumed.

Mr. SHERMAN, of Connecticut, was for leaving the clause as it stands. He disapproved of the Slave-trade ; yet as the States were now possessed of the right to import slaves, as the public good did not require it to be taken from them, and as it was expedient to have as few objections as possible to the proposed scheme of government, he thought it best to leave the matter as we find it. He observed that the abolition of Slavery seemed to be going on in the United Sates, and that the good sense of the several States would probably by degrees complete it. He urged on the Convention the necessity of dispatching its business.

Col. MASON, of Virginia—This infernal traffic originated in the avarice of British merchants. The British Government constantly checked the attempts of Virginia to put a stop to it. *The present question concerns not the importing States alone, but the whole Union.* The evil of having slaves was experienced during the late war. Had slaves been treated as they might have been by the enemy, they would have proved dangerous instruments in their hands. But their folly dealt by the slaves as it did by the tories. He mentioned the dangerous insurrections of the slaves in Greece and Sicily ; and the instructions given by CROMWELL to the Commissioners sent to Virginia, to arm the servants and slaves in case other means of obtaining its submission should fail. Maryland and Virginia, he said, had already prohibited the importation of slaves expressly. North Carolina had done the same in substance. All this would be in vain, if South Carolina and Georgia be at liberty to import. The Western people are already calling out for slaves for their new lands, and will fill that country with slaves, if they can be got through South Carolina and Georgia. Slavery discourages arts and manufactures. The poor despise labor when performed by slaves. They prevent the emigration of whites, who really enrich and strengthen the country. They produce the most pernicious effects on manners. Every master of slaves is born a petty tyrant. They bring the judgment of Heaven on a country. As nations cannot be rewarded or punished in the next world, they must be in this. By an inevitable chain of causes and effects, Providence punishes national sins by national calamities. He lamented that some of our Eastern brethren had, from a lust of gain, embarked in this nefarious traffic. As to the States being in possession of the right to import, this was the case with many other rights, properly to be given up. He held it essential in every point of view, that the General Government should have power to prevent the increase of Slavery.

Mr. ELLSWORTH, of Connecticut, as he had never owned a slave, could not judge of the effects of Slavery on character. He said, however, that if it was to be considered in a moral light, we ought to go further and free those already in the country. As slaves also multiply so fast in Virginia and Maryland that it is cheaper to raise than import them, whilst in the sickly rice swamps foreign supplies are necessary, if we go no further than is urged, we shall be unjust towards South Carolina and Georgia. Let us not intermeddle. As population increases poor laborers will be so plenty as to render slaves useless. *Slavery, in time, will not be a speck in our country.* Provision is already made in Connecticut for abolishing it, and the abolition has already taken place in Massachusetts. As to the danger of insurrection from foreign influence, that will become a motive of kind treatment of the slaves.

Mr. PINCKNEY, of South Carolina—If Slavery be wrong, it is justified by the example of all the world. He cited the case of Greece, Rome and the other ancient States—the sanction given by France, Holland and other modern States. In all ages one-half of mankind had been slaves. *If the Southern States were let alone, they will probably of themselves stop importations.* He would, himself, as a citizen of South Carolina, vote for it. An attempt to take away the right, as proposed, *will produce serious objections to the Constitution, which* he wished to see adopted.

Gen. PINCKNEY, of South Carolina, declared it to be his firm opinion that if himself and all his colleagues were to sign the Constitution and use their personal influence, it would be of no avail towards obtaining the assent of their constituents. *South Carolina and Georgia cannot do without slaves.* As to Virginia, she will gain by stopping the importations. Her slaves will rise in value, and she has more than she wants. It would be unequal to require South Carolina and Georgia to confederate on such unequal terms. He said the royal assent before the Revolution, had never been refused to South Carolina, as to Virginia. He contended that the importation of slaves would be for the interest of the whole Union. The more slaves the more produce to employ the carrying trade; the more consumption also, and the more of this, the more revenue for the common treasury. He admitted it to be reasonable that slaves should be dutied like other imports; but should consider a rejection of the clause as an exclusion of South Carolina from the Union.

Mr. BALDWIN, of Georgia, had conceived national objects alone to be before the Convention; not such as, like the present, were of a local nature. *Georgia was decided on this point.* That State has always hitherto supposed a General Government to be the pursuit of the central States, who wished to have a vortex for everything; that her distance would preclude her from equal advantage; and that she could not prudently purchase it by yielding national powers. From this it might be understood in what light she would view an attempt to abridge one of her favorite prerogatives. *If left to herself she may probably put a stop to the evil.* As one ground for this conjecture, he took notice of the sect of — which he said was a respectable class of people, who carried their ethics beyond the mere *equality of men,* extending their humanity to the claims of the whole animal creation.

Mr. WILSON, of Pennsylvania, observed that if South Carolina and Georgia were themselves disposed to get rid of the importation of slaves in a short time, as had been suggested, they would never refuse to unite because the importation might be prohibited. As the section now stands, all articles imported are to be taxed. *Slaves alone are exempt.* This is in fact a bounty on that article.

Mr. GERRY, of Massachusetts, thought we had nothing to do with the conduct of the States as to slaves, *but ought to be careful not to give any sanction to it.*

Mr. DICKINSON, of Delaware, considered it as inadmissible, on every principle of honor and safety, that the importation of slaves should be authorized to the States by the Constitution. *The true question was, whether the national happiness would be promoted or impeded by the importation* ; and this ought to be left to the National Government, not to the States particularly interested. If England and France permit Slavery, slaves are, at the same time, excluded from both these kingdoms. Greece and Rome were made unhappy by their slaves. He could not believe that the Southern States would refuse to confederate on the account apprehended; especially as the power was not likely to be immediately exercised by the General Government.

Mr. WILLIAMSON, of North Carolina, stated the law of North Carolina on the subject, to wit : that it did not directly prohibit the importation of slaves. It imposed a duty of £5 on each slave imported from Africa ; £10 on each from elsewhere ; and £50 on each from a State licensing manumission. He thought the Southern States could not be members of the Union, if the clause should be rejected ; and that it was wrong to force anything down not absolutely necessary, and which any State must disagree to.

Mr. KING, of Massachusetts, thought the subject should be considered in a political light only. If two States will not agree to the Constitution, as stated on one side, he could affirm with equal belief, on the other, that great and equal opposition would be experienced from the other States. He remarked on the exemption of slaves from duty, whilst every other import was subjected to it, as an inequality that could not fail to strike the commercial sagacity of the Northern and Middle States.

Mr. LANGDON, of New-Hampshire, was *strenuous for giving the power to the General Government. He could not, with a good conscience, leave it with the States, who could then go on with the traffic, without being re-* strained by the opinions here given, that they will themselves cease to import slaves.

Gen. PINCKNEY, of South Carolina, thought himself bound to declare candidly, that he did not think South Carolina would stop her importations of slaves in any short time ; but only stop them occasionally, as she now does. He moved to commit the clause that slaves might be made liable to an equal tax with other imports, which he thought right, and which would remove one difficulty that had been started.

Mr. RUTLEDGE, of South Carolina—*If the Convention thinks that North Carolina, South Carolina and Georgia will ever agree to the plan, unless their right to import slaves be untouched, the expectation is vain.* The people of those States will never be such fools as to give up so important an interest. He was strenuous against striking out the section, and seconded the motion of Gen. PINCKNEY for a commitment.

Mr. GOUVERNEUR MORRIS, of Pennsylvania, wished the whole subject to be committed, including the clause relating to taxes on exports and to a navigation act. These things may form a bargain among the Northern and Southern States.

Mr. BUTLER, of Georgia, declared that he never would agree to the power of taxing exports.

Mr. SHERMAN, of Connecticut, said *it was better to let the Southern States import slaves than to part with them, if they made that a sine qua non.* He was opposed to a tax on slaves imported, as making the matter worse because it implied they were *property.* He acknowledged that if the power of prohibiting the importation should be given to the General Government, it would be exercised. He thought it would be its duty to exercise the power.

Mr. REED, of Delaware, was for the commitment, provided the clause concerning taxes on exports should also be committed.

Mr. SHERMAN, of Connecticut, observed that that clause had been agreed to, and therefore could not be committed.

Mr. RANDOLPH, of Virginia, was for committing, in order that some middle ground might, if possible, be found. He could never agree to the clause as it stands. *He would sooner risk the Constitution.* He dwelt on the dilemma to which the Convention was exposed. By agreeing to the clause, it would revolt the Quakers, the Methodists, and many others in the States having no slaves. On the other hand, two States might be lost to the Union. Let us, then, he said, try the chance of a commitment.

On the question for committing the remaining part of sections 4 and 5 of article 7 : Connecticut, New-Jersey, Maryland, Virginia, North Carolina, South Carolina, Georgia—Aye 7 ; New-Hampshire, Pennsylvania, Delaware—No, 3 ; Massachusetts, absent.

[The whole subject was thus recommitted for the purpose of coming to some compromise.]

From Madison Papers, Vol. III., p. 1,415.

FRIDAY, Aug. 24.

Gov. LIVINGSTON, of New-Jersey, from the Committee of Eleven, delivered the following report :

" Strike out so much of the 4th section as was referred to the Committee, and insert, ' The migration or importation of such persons as the several States now existing shall think proper to admit, shall not be prohibited by the Legislature prior to the year 1800.'"

From page 1,427.

SATURDAY, Aug. 25.

The Report of the Committee of Eleven being taken up,

Gen. PINCKNEY, of South Carolina, moved to strike out the words, "the year eighteen hundred," as the year limiting the importation of slaves, and to insert the words, " the year eighteen hundred and eight."

Mr. GORHAM, of Massachusetts, seconded the motion.

Mr. MADISON, of Virginia—Twenty years will produce all the mischief that can be apprehended from the liberty to import slaves. So long a term will be more dishonorable to the American character, than to say nothing about it in the Constitution.

On the motion, which passed in the affirmative, New-Hampshire, Massachusetts, Connecticut, Maryland, North Carolina, South Carolina, Georgia—Aye, 7 ; New-Jersey, Pennsylvania, Delaware, Virginia—No, 4.

Mr. GOUVERNEUR MORRIS, of Pennsylvania, was for

making the clause read at once, "the importation of slaves into North Carolina, South Carolina and Georgia shall not be prohibited, &c." This, he said, would be most fair, and would avoid the ambiguity by which, under the power with regard to naturalization, the liberty reserved to the States might be defeated. *He wished it to be known, also, that this part of the Constitution was a compliance with those States.* If the change of language, however, should be objected to by the members from those States, he should not urge it.

Col. MASON, of Virginia, was not against using the term "slaves," but against naming North Carolina, South Carolina and Georgia, *lest it should give offence to the people of those States.*

Mr. SHERMAN, of Connecticut, liked a description better than the term proposed, which had been declined by the old Congress, and were not pleasing to some people.

Mr. CLYMER, of Pennsylvania, concurred with Mr. SHERMAN.

Mr. WILLIAMSON, of North Carolina, said that both in opinion and practice, he was against Slavery, but thought it more in favor of humanity, from a view of all circumstances, *to let in South Carolina and Georgia on those terms than to exclude them from the Union.*

Mr. GOVERNEUR MORRIS, of Pennsylvania, withdrew his motion.

Mr. DICKINSON wished the clause to be confined to the States, which had not themselves prohibited the importation of slaves, and for that purpose moved to amend the clause, so as to read : " The importation of slaves into such of the States as shall permit the same, shall not be prohibited by the Legislature of the United States until the year 1808"—which was disagreed to *nem con.*

The first part of the report was then agreed to, amended as follows : " The migration or importation of such persons as the several States now existing shall think proper to admit, shall not be prohibited by the Legislature prior to the year 1808."

New-Hampshire, Massachusetts, Connecticut, Maryland, North Carolina, South Carolina, Georgia— Aye, 7 ; New-Jersey, Pennsylvania, Delaware, Virginia—No, 4.

———o———

Mr. Yancey's Letter on the Prohibition of the Slave-trade.

MR. YANCEY AND HIS ACCUSERS.

From the New-York (Sunday) Herald, Nov. 18.

MONTGOMERY, Ala., Nov. 9, 1860.

To the Editor of the Herald :

Since my return home my attention has been called to an editorial article in the NEW YORK TIMES, of Oct. 27, headed, " Mr. YANCEY on Matters of Fact —The North and the Slave-trade." The article purports to be a reply to assertions made in my speeches in New-York and Boston. Their substance will be found in the following quotations from those speeches. In my speech in New-York I said :

" Our forefathers were not only slaveholders, but imported slaves from Africa. Virginia wished to suppress the trade, but Massachusetts and other States wished it to be carried on. [Laughter.] Massachusetts and those other States insisted that the Slave-trade should not be prohibited by any act of Congress, and resisted all attempts to prohibit it until the act of Congress of 1808 was passed ; for, by an article of the Constitution, which was beyond the reach of Congressional amendment, it was provided by our forefathers that no change should be made in the Slave-trade until the year 1808. How did that sound with the modern theorists as to the existence of an irrepressible conflict ?" [Applause.]

In my speech at Boston, I said :

" Well, then, your fathers, in demanding that the Slave-trade, which existed when the Declaration of Independence was made, should be continued ; in demanding that the institution of Slavery, which existed when the Constitution was formed, should have a wider basis ; in demanding that slaves should be increased in number ; in demanding that they should have the privilege of trading in them, of buying them and selling them to our people—I ask you now candidly, did they not, in demanding all this, demand of their posterity perfect good faith in securing the title to that property ?" [" No !" " Yes !"]

The editor of the *Times* asserts that " these statements show that the disunion orator is either very imperfectly read in the history of our country, or very reckless and unscrupulous in the statement of facts." The whole tenor and spirit of the article can be best shown by the following extract :

" It is true, as he alleges, that Virginia was opposed to the continuance of the Slave-trade, and we are sorry to say that this is the only truth contained in the statement."

The editor then proceeds to give garbled extracts from the debates in the Federal Convention, and adds his own weak attempts at argument to sustain his sweeping assertion. As the point made by me is one of some importance in the present aspect of political affairs, I ask the use of your almost universally read columns to spread my reply before the public. Analyze my statements and they will be found to consist of the following points :

1. The Slave-trade existed when the Declaration of Independence was made.

2. Virginia desired to have that trade suppressed.

3. " Massachusetts and other States wished it to be carried on."

4. No change was to be made in the Slave-trade provision in the Constitution prior to the year 1808.

These are the only matters stated as facts, and the truth of each and all, excepting that numbered two, is unqualifiedly denied by the editor of the NEW-YORK TIMES. I might afford to leave the ignorance or mendacity of the editor of the TIMES to be judged of by the public intelligence as to the first statement made by me ; but as I have before me the " Debates in the Federal Convention," from which he has made his quotations, I will simply refer him to the 3d volume of the *Madison Papers,* page 1,389, on which will be found Mr. SHERMAN'S (of Connecticut) statement—" As the States are now possessed of the right to import slaves, as the public good did not require it to be taken from them, &c., he thought it best to leave the matter as we find it." In sustaining my position, numbered three and four, I shall cite not merely what was said by certain delegates from some of the States, but also what is far more pertinent to the argument—what the States did—what they voted for and obtained. That is to be taken as the highest evidence of what each State wished to record as its will and decision.

By reference to *Madison's Papers,* vol. 2, p. 1,226, the draft of a constitution will be found as reported by the Committee of Detail. It did not provide for a prohibition or tax on the importation of slaves. On this a debate sprang up. I quote from that debate the views of leading delegates :

Mr. L. MARTIN, of Maryland, proposed to vary article 7, section 4, so as to allow a prohibition or tax on the importation of slaves. (Vol. 3, p. 1,388.)

Mr. ELLSWORTH, of Connecticut, was for leaving the clause as it stands. Let every State import what it pleases. The morality or wisdom of Slavery are considerations belonging to the States themselves. (Vol. 3, p. 1,380.)

Mr. SHERMAN, of Connecticut, was for leaving the clause as it stands. (Vol. 3, p. 1,390.)

Col. MASON, of Virginia—He lamented that some of our Eastern brethren had, from a lust of gain, embarked in this nefarious traffic. He held it essential, in every point of view, that the General Government should have the power to prevent the increase of Slavery. (3d vol., p. 1,390-1.)

Mr. ELLSWORTH, of Connecticut—He said, however, that if it was to be considered in a moral light, we ought to go further, and free those already in the country. As slaves also multiply so fast in Virginia and Maryland that it is cheaper to raise than import them, whilst in the sickly rice swamps foreign supplies are necessary. If we go further than is urged, we shall be unjust towards South Carolina and Georgia. Let us not intermeddle. (3d vol., p. 1,391.)

Mr. KING, of Massachusets, thought the subject should be considered in a political light only. * * * He remarked on the exemption of slaves from duty, whilst every other import was subjected to it, as an inequality that could not fail to strike the commercial sagacity of the Northern and Middle States. (3d vol, p. 1,394.)

Mr. GOUVERNEUR MORRIS, of Pennsylvania, wished

the whole subject to be committed, including the clause on imports. These things may form a bargain among the Southern and Northern States, (3d vol., p. 1,395.)

The matter was committed. The Committee made report in substance as the section now stands in the Constitution, excepting that the Committee reported in favor of the year 1800.

Gen. PINCKNEY, of South Carolina, moved to substitute 1808 for 1800. (3d vol., p. 1,427.)

Mr. GORHAM, of Massachusetts, seconded the motion.

Mr. MADISON, of Virginia—Twenty years will produce all the mischief that can be apprehended from the liberty to import slaves.

On the motion, which passed on the affirmative, New-Hampshire, Connecticut, Massachusetts and three other States, Aye. New-Jersey, Pennsylvania, Delaware and Virginia, No. (3d vol., p. 1,427.)

The first part of the report was then agreed to as amended, as follows: The migration or importation of such persons as the several States now existing shall think proper to admit shall not be prohibited prior to the year 1808. New-Hampshire, Massachusetts, Connecticut, Maryland, North Carolina, South Carolina, Georgia, Aye—7. New-Jersey, Pennsylvania, Delaware, Virginia, No—4. (3d vol., pp. 1,428 and 1,429.)

The above extracts of opinions of leading Northern Delegates, and the above-cited votes of Massachusetts, Connecticut, and other States, prove my statement numbered 3. It proves that the proposition for "prohibition" of the "importation of slaves" came from Maryland, and was warmly supported, on moral grounds, by Virginia, and that Connecticut immediately pronounced: "Let every State import what it pleases;" while Massachusetts ably seconded Connecticut, that it was "to be considered in a political light only," and at once suggested the exemption of imported slaves from duty, however "struck the commercial sagacity" of the North. He made it a subject for trade, not for moral speculations. Those extracts and votes also prove that when the Committee reported the year 1800 as the period within which the trade should not be prohibited, Massachusetts promptly seconded and acted with South Carolina in a successful effort to extend the time for the importation of slaves from Africa to the year 1808.

I now turn to the consideration of the fourth statement made by me, and I continue extracts from the debates in the Federal Convention:

Mr. GERRY, of Massachusetts, moved to reconsider article 19, viz.: "On application of two-thirds of the States in this Union for an amendment of this Constitution, the Legislature of the United States shall call a Convention for that purpose." He said: "Two-thirds may obtain a Convention, a majority of which can bind the Union to innovations that may subvert the State Constitutions altogether."

On Mr. GERRY's motion, Massachusetts, Connecticut, Pennsylvania and six other States voted Aye. (3d vol., p. 1,103-4-5.)

It being reconsidered, Mr. RUTLEDGE, of South Carolina, said "he never could agree to give a power by which the articles relating to slaves might be altered by the States not interested in that property, and prejudiced against it." In order to obviate that objection, these words were added to the proposition —"Provided that no amendment which may be made prior to the year 1808 shall in any manner affect the fourth and fifth sections of the seventh article." On this, which passed in the affirmative, the vote stood thus—Massachusetts, Connecticut, New-Jersey, Pennsylvania, Maryland, Virginia, North Carolina, South Carolina, Georgia—Aye. Delaware—No. New-Hampshire, divided.

These extracts and votes prove my fourth proposition or statement, and that after Massachusetts had seconded and voted for the section to extend the time for importation of slaves, she also called for the reconsideration of the article upon the mode of amending the Constitution, and voted for the clause that no amendment to be made should affect in any way the Slave-trade guaranty. I have nothing more to add. Having now corrected the hostile and malignant criticisms of two leading editors in the Black Republican cause, viz.: Mr. THURLOW WEED and Mr. HENRY J. RAYMOND—the first in my speech at Rochester, and the last in this letter, I leave the whole subject of those speeches to the judgment of an intelligent public. I may be permitted to observe, however, that I have not had an opportunity of correcting the reports which were made of them; and there are errors of style and statement in the reports which I should have been glad to have corrected.

Could those papers which have copied the TIMES' article do me the justice to publish my reply, I should be gratified by that act of courtesy, while, at the same time, the cause of truth would be subserved.

Your obedient servant,   W. L. YANCEY.

II.

THE MOTIVES AND OBJECTS OF THE DISUNION MOVEMENT.

NEW-YORK, Nov. 26, 1860.

In a former letter I corrected the misrepresentations, historical and statistical, by which you endeavored to convince the people of the Northern States that they ought to permit the indefinite *increase of Slavery.* I propose now to consider the bearing of that argument upon the present Disunion movement.

You are urging the State of Alabama to secede from the Union,—or, if she will not take the lead in secession, to join any other State that may do so. What you advise her to do, you think every slaveholding State should do also,—but you are unwilling to trust the decision of the question to the voice of all those States, assembled in Convention and acting together,—or even to the calm judgment and consenting action of the Cotton States alone. You insist that some one State shall withdraw from the Union by herself, trusting that the community of interest, the pride and the

commitments of the other Cotton States will impel them, not only to imitate her example, but to come to her aid, in resisting any armed attempt of the Federal Government to support the Constitution and maintain the integrity of the Union.

I am constrained by the evidence of events to confess that your efforts have been crowned with a startling degree of success. Although the final step has not yet been taken by any State, public sentiment in three or four of them seems quite prepared to take it. The machinery which you organized some years since for the purpose of "firing the Southern heart, instructing the Southern mind, and giving courage to each other," has done its work far more effectually than even you could have anticipated;—and that "Proper Moment," when, as you declared in your letter of June 15, 1858, you could "by one organized concerted action, *precipitate the Cotton States into a revolution,*" seems in very truth to have arrived. Gladly as I would shut my eyes to so unwelcome a fact I cannot doubt that an overwhelming majority of the people of South Carolina are prepared for secession,—and that after the blow has once been struck there is much reason to believe that a majority of the people in Georgia, Alabama and Mississippi will rally, in arms if necessary, to her support.

What is likely to be the result of such a movement, I may perhaps consider before I close this correspondence. At present my purpose is rather to examine its motives.

The great mass of the people in the Cotton growing States are imbued with the general conviction that their separation from the Union is desirable : —and the same thing is true, though to a much less extent, of the people in the other Slaveholding States. If we were to ask them what are the reasons for such a conviction,—what are the precise wrongs which they have suffered under the Union, and what the advantages they expect to secure for themselves by leaving it,—we should receive very different answers from different States. The motives which influence Disunionists in Alabama and South Carolina, are not the motives which influence Disunionists in Maryland and Virginia. All would agree that their common institution—Slavery—is in some way menaced by the Government as it now exists, and especially as it will exist after it passes into the hands of the Republican Party ;—but they would differ as to the shape which its perils assume. In order to ascertain the real motive of disunion, therefore, we must go to those few leading minds with whom, like all great movements, it had its origin. Less than two years before the Declaration of Independence was issued, WASHINGTON expressed the sentiment of the great body of the people when he declared that the Colonies had no thought or desire to sever their connection with the mother country. But SAMUEL ADAMS, and JAMES OTIS, and JOHN ADAMS, and PATRICK HENRY, knew five years before, that independence was the real object, and would be the crowning consummation of the current popular protests against English rule.

The disunion movement has been set on foot by a comparatively small number of men in the Southern States. Mr. CALHOUN planted the seeds of it, in the intellects and the ambition of the most prominent and influential of the rising statesmen of the South. His doctrines found no lodgment in the popular mind. His arguments were too abstract for general appreciation, and the idea of disunion was never popular out of South Carolina, during his lifetime. Since his death the apostles of his creed have been untiring in its propagation ;—and no one man has been more zealous than yourself in this work. You have been, moreover, somewhat bolder and more frank in the application of his theories to the practical policy of the country,—you have been more willing than many of those who were working with you, to avow and advocate the measures which those

theories were intended to support. I feel justified, therefore, in regarding you as the best representative of the disunion movement, and in seeking the causes of that movement, in your opinions and declarations.

What, then, are *your* reasons for urging a dissolution of the Union ?

ELECTION OF A REPUBLICAN PRESIDENT.

If I were to ask every Disunionist in the South this question, nine-tenths of them would probably reply, the election of LINCOLN and the triumph of the Republican party. But you know that in and of itself this constitutes no justification whatever. You claim that Secession is strictly a constitutional proceeding. But certainly it is not more so than the election of a President in strict compliance with every form and every requirement of the Constitution. You say he has been elected by a sectional vote. Admit the fact ;—that does not make it one whit the less Constitutional. The Constitution knows nothing of *sections* in the Union,—either as elements of power or as the claimants of rights. It recognizes only States and People,—and it assigns to each their just proportion of power in the election of a President, as in every other function of government. The States have an equality in the Electoral college to the extent of two votes each :—and then each State has an additional weight in proportion to its population. This provision, which the Constitution deemed sufficient to secure the individual States from injustice, has been fully complied with. The election of LINCOLN involves not the slightest departure from the Constitution in any particular. If secession were equally Constitutional, your right to secede would be beyond question.

But he is elected by the Republican Party—and by a minority of the popular vote, through the divisions of his opponents. True—but Republicans are *people* ; a Constitutional majority, composed wholly of Republicans, is not one whit the less a Constitutional majority of the people than if it were composed in part of others : and a *Constitutional* majority—not an absolute, numerical majority—is all that is required for the election of a President. It is a maxim of law, moreover, as well as of common sense, applicable to public as well as to private controversies, that no man shall take advantage of his own wrong : and those who are now Disunionists in the South, with you at their head, are directly responsible for that rupture of the Democratic Party which aided, if it did not cause, the election of LINCOLN.

These, you will say, are technical reasons against secession. True, and they are only assigned in answer to technical reasons in its favor. If you stand upon the Constitution, and assert your right under it to secede in case of its violation, I am free to show that no such violation has taken place, and that you have, therefore, no such right.

Nor can you find any pretext for secession in the character of the man thus elected. If you have made yourself at all familiar with it—as you are bound to do before making it the ground of objection—you must know that the Union contains no purer, no more upright, no more patriotic citizen ; no man more just and fair-minded, more certain to discharge the duties of his office with scrupulous regard to the rights of all, than Mr. LINCOLN. But even if this were not so, I understand you to have expressly waived this as a reason for secession, in your speech at Montgomery in 1858, where I find you saying :

" If I understand my distinguished friend from Virginia, (Mr. PRYOR,) the election of a Black Republican President would be an issue for disunion. I understand my learned colleague (Mr. HILLARD) to say that upon that issue he would be ready to dissolve the Union. I say with all deference to my colleagues here, *that no more inferior issue could be tendered to the South upon which we should dissolve the Union than the loss of an election.* If in the contest of 1860 for the Presidency, SEWARD should receive the legal number of votes necessary to elect him according to the forms of the Constitution and laws, gentlemen say that then will be the time to dissolve the Union. If that is made the cause of disunion, I say to them that I will go with them, but I will feel that *I am going in the wake of an inferior issue,* that there was a banner over me that is not of the kind I would wish. When I am asked to raise the flag of revolution against an election under the forms of law and the Constitution, *I am asked to do an unconstitutional thing,* according to the Constitution as it now exists. *I am asked to put myself in the position of a rebel, of a traitor* ; in a position where, if the Government should succeed and put down the revolution, *I and my friends can be arraigned before the Supreme Court of the United States, and there be sentenced to be hanged for violating the Constitution and laws of my country.*"

The fact, therefore, that a Republican President has been elected cannot be your reason for disunion. As a symptom and precursor of other events it might have more weight. If there were any substantial reason for supposing that Mr. LINCOLN would aid or countenance any infraction of Southern rights, any trespass upon Southern interests, any attempt to disturb the public peace in the Southern States, you would be quite right in putting the South in an attitude of defence, and of preparation for resistance, to any extent which the injustice, when it should come, might require. But it is scarcely becoming a great and brave people, to act upon a mere apprehension of dangers that may never arrive ; and in this case you have every assurance which Mr. LINCOLN'S declared sentiments and which the necessities of his position can give, that no trespass upon Southern rights will be permitted which he has the power to prevent.

You fear that, whatever his personal opinions and purposes may be, he will be governed by the requirements of his party. But you have seen enough of public life to know that seeking power against a party in possession is one thing, and wielding it under all the responsibilities which it involves, is quite another. The Republican Party will now have far more interest than any other in preventing renewals of the John Brown raid,—in punishing every movement against the peace of a Southern State,—in enforcing the laws, suppressing everything like resistance to their execution, and securing that public tranquillity which rests upon

justice and equal rights. You mistake the North in supposing that the election of LINCOLN indicates any disposition on the part of the people to countenance any infraction of Southern rights. They elected him because they did not believe he had the slightest sympathy with any such purpose,—and because they knew that the public welfare imperatively demanded a change in the spirit and tone of the Federal Councils. And if the Republican Administration should tolerate the least invasion of Southern rights, the very first elections would deprive it of the support of every considerable Northern State.

If, therefore, you had no stronger reason than the election of a Republican President, I am sure you would not urge the secession of the Southern States.

SURRENDER OF FUGITIVE SLAVES.

The refusal to surrender fugitive slaves,—and especially the enactment by several Northern States of Personal Liberty bills, with the apparent intent to prevent their recovery, is much more generally assigned as a reason for Disunion. But this cannot be your motive, nor that of the Gulf States whose action will dissolve the Union, if it is dissolved at all ;—for they suffer scarcely any practical inconvenience from this source. Out of the eleven hundred slaves who escape from the South annually, I presume that all the Cotton States together do not lose *fifty.* Virginia, Maryland and Kentucky are the States upon whom this wrong and this loss fall ; yet they are Union States. They have so little sympathy with the secession movement that you will not trust yourself in Convention with them,—and the Disunionists of South Carolina insultingly repel all advice or counsel from them on this subject. You must be aware, moreover, that the Supreme Court has released the States from all obligation to return fugitive slaves by devolving that duty upon the Federal Government ;—that the law of 1850, in fulfillment of that duty, by its defective provision for proofs of identity, subjects free citizens of Northern States to the danger of being carried into Slavery, as has happened once at least since its enactment ;—and that the professed object of these Personal Liberty bills has been to protect free citizens from that peril, and not to prevent the return of actual fugitives. The injustice which they may work to the owners of fugitive slaves, is not greater than the injustice which may arise to free men from the harsh and unguarded execution of the Fugitive Slave law.

I am not disposed, however, to enter upon any vindication of the general policy of these bills. I have always opposed them as at war in their spirit, with the constitutional obligation to surrender fugitive slaves, and as calculated needlessly to exasperate the people of the Southern States. Their enactment has been usually due to the race of rival partisans for local popularity. It has been part of the machinery of our political contests :

11

and as a matter of practical importance I presume I am quite right in saying, that all the Personal Liberty bills that have been passed in all the States, have never released half-a-dozen fugitives from the service from which they had escaped. I am quite sure that none of the Southern States would dream of secession on account of the actual injury they sustain from these Personal Liberty bills, in the loss of their fugitive slaves; for if that were the motive of secession it would not be most powerful where the injury is the least. In that case, Kentucky, and not South Carolina, would take the lead in the movement of Disunion.

You say the passage of these bills is insulting to the South—an outrage upon her rights and a mockery of her sufferings. I do not deny it. I admit that there has been a great deal too much that is offensive to Southern feeling in the action of the North upon this subject. But has all the insult been upon one side in this matter? Have the Constitutional rights of Northern men—their right to "life, liberty and the pursuit of happiness"— always been respected in the South? I merely suggest this point as worthy your consideration, if you propose to dissolve the Union because you have been insulted. We have quite as much ground of complaint on this score as you have. Neither section has been blameless. Both have steps to retrace and reforms to practice; and I think you will find the North quite ready to meet the South at least half way in this matter.

THE TERRITORIAL QUESTION.

But you claim the right to carry Slavery into the Territories, and that position, you say, is denied by the Republican Party. The assertion of *the right* is one thing,—and its exercise is quite another. I think I run no risk of contradiction when I say, that the present holders of slaves in the Southern States care nothing about the *exercise* of the right asserted on their behalf. They do not wish to go to the Territories themselves,—still less to take their slaves with them. There are no territories now belonging to the Union into which slaves could be carried without a prodigious sacrifice of their value. What slave-owner in Alabama will take slaves worth from $1,000 to $1,500 there into Kansas or New-Mexico, where they are not worth, either for sale or for hire, one-half of that amount,—to say nothing of the risk of losing them? Mr. GAULDEN, of Georgia, was quite right when he told the Charleston Convention that the *South had no slaves to send into the territories,—* she had not enough to supply the demand for labor at home. She needs on her own plantations all the slave-labor she can possibly command,— and any attempt to send slaves into the territories would only diminish her product of cotton, weaken her domestic strength and add nothing to her wealth elsewhere. Nor are the political consider. ations which the question involves likely to change her action. For if she should send slaves into any territory in order to make it a slave territory, she must draw additional supplies from Maryland, Del-

aware or Virginia and thus do all in her power to convert them into free States. The South never can colonize the territories with slaves, until she can be at liberty to increase her supply by importation from abroad.

There was a time when the question of Slavery in the Territories was the paramount political question of the day. I think that time has passed; and that it can never come up again, as a practical question, until after the African Slave-trade has been reopened. The Gulf States will send no slaves to Kansas or New-Mexico so long as they command such enormous prices at home ;—nor will Virginia or Kentucky send slaves thither, so long as their prices rule three times as high in the markets at their doors. Slaveholders who emigrate into new regions first sell their slaves, and thus take their property with them in the shape of cash. As you clearly expressed it in your Montgomery speech :

"*Slaves are too valuable to be risked in a contest with Free-Soil-dom in any of our new Territories.* The consequence is that this species of property is kept in the States which protect it, and where there is a demand for it.*"

Practically, therefore, we shall hear nothing more of the Territorial question until the greater question which lies behind it, and gives it all its importance, shall have been decided. And this, I think, is the general conviction of the reflecting portion of the people of the North, even among the Republican Party. Mr. SEWARD, you will remember, in one of his campaign speeches, said he considered it settled that there would be no further extension of Slavery into the Territories until the African Slave-trade should be restored : and it cannot have escaped your observation that the Republican Convention at Chicago held language on this point very different from that used at Philadelphia in 1856. As things now stand, I believe the North would lose nothing whatever by leaving the whole subject of extending Slavery into the Territories entirely untouched ;—and in the absence of any further causes of irritation from the South, I think it not at all unlikely that the North would consent that the question should be decided by the course of events and the natural influences of climate and emigration. If I held any official position, or any post which would involve any party in the responsibility for these opinions, I might not hazard such an expression of them. But I give it as my own judgment, based upon the grounds I have already mentioned.

But suppose this to be true. Suppose the incoming Administration should decide to leave this whole matter precisely where it stands at present, making no attempt to prohibit by law the extension of Slavery into the Territories, conceding that the inhabitants may, when they come to form a State Constitution, and not before, admit or exclude Slavery in their own discretion, and agreeing to admit the State into the Union in either case :— would the South accept that as a final adjustment of the differences between the two sections?

Would you,—and those who are acting with you in the disunion movement?

I think you would reply : "*Yes*, if you will concede it as a matter of *Right*, of principle, with whatever logical consequences that principle may involve. But if it is offered on grounds of expediency alone—as a practical solution of an embarrassing question—*No*." What the South contends for is the *principle* that her slaves are property in the view of the Constitution—to be held, treated, and in all respects regarded by the Federal Government, as property, and nothing else, precisely like horses, cattle, and other movable chattels. It is the absolute indefeasible *Right* itself, and not the *exercise* of the right, which the South would demand as the price of her remaining in the Union.

STATE EQUALITY AND THE SLAVE-TRADE.

Now, why do you make this distinction? Why would you refuse the privilege of carrying slaves into the Territories, unless you could secure at the same time the absolute *right* to do so? Because the former would be valueless without the latter, Because you have no slaves to take into the Territories,—and you need the *right*,—and the principle on which it rests, in order to get them, and thus render the concession itself of any practical value. In other words, you require the restoration of the African Slave-trade, in order to extend Slavery into the Territories. The recognition of the principle you contend for will give you both :—while the bare concession of the extension itself will secure you neither.

The principle you assert is the absolute equality of the States in regard to the tenure of property, —that each State shall be allowed to make its own laws concerning property,—the ownership of persons or of things,—and that any right of property which any State may see fit thus to create, shall be recognized by the Federal Government as absolute and indefeasible.

This is what you understand by the Equality of the States. You will concede, I think, that I do not state the claim too broadly. Any restriction of it,—anything less than is included in it, defeats the purpose for which it is put forward. But suppose it to be conceded. It follows, of course, that any person may do what he pleases with his property. He may hold it,—or buy and sell it,— wherever the jurisdiction of the Constitution extends, and the Federal Government is bound to protect him in so doing. Whatever I may do with broadcloth, you may do with a negro slave,—anywhere within the jurisdiction of the Federal Constitution,—if that Constitution, as you contend, puts the two upon the same footing. All the property of all the States,—whatever any State chooses to make property by her local laws,—becomes property in the eye of the Federal Constitution, and consequently becomes the subject of Commerce,— domestic, or foreign, at the will of its owner,—subject only to such uniform laws as may be adopted for all property, in the regulation of commerce, between the States or with foreign nations.

How far the practical application of this principle would affect the general subject of property, the purpose of this correspondence does not lead me, nor do its limits permit me, to inquire. It would evidently *put the whole matter of property under the control of any one State*,—and each State would be sovereign *quoad hoc*, not only over its own affairs, but over the affairs of all the other States. That the principle would involve the restoration of the foreign trade in slaves, if any State should choose to enter upon it, you will not deny, nor have I the slightest doubt. Indeed, in your Montgomery speech you took precisely this ground, and denounced the laws of Congress prohibiting the Slave-trade as unconstitutional, because they denied and destroyed this principle of the Equality of the States. You say :

" The laws prohibiting the foreign Slave-trade, are in violation of the spirit of the Constitution, and are unjust and an insult to the South, and ought to be repealed. * * * *What right has this Government to discriminate against one of the States in the Union that has equal rights in the Union ?* Where will you find the right in the Constitution? Nowhere. Will my friend from Virginia (Mr. PRYOR) find in any clause of the Constitution any enactment against the Slave-trade? No, he will not find it there. What will he find in that Constitution? He will find simply this : ' Congress shall enact no law prohibiting the migration or importation of such persons as any of the States may see fit to admit before the year 1808.' What do you call that? Why that is one of the Constitutional guarantees of the Slave-trade. * * * In 1807 a law was enacted making it a misdemeanor to import a slave from abroad. Now I ask every sensible man in this Convention, *was not that statute a violation of the spirit of the Constitution ?* What was the spirit of the Constitution? It was that African Slavery within our dominions was legal, and *that we stood upon an equal footing with all the rest of the States with reference to this species of property*. And what became of our equality when the law was passed that said, you of the South shall not import negroes from Africa, though you of the North may import jackasses from Malta? *What became of our equality then ?* A blow was struck against it, when this Government passed a law discriminating against the slave labor of the South. * * * *The law struck at the equality of the South.* If so, it follows as plainly, as that two and two make four, that the law is an *unconstitutional law.* Is there any gentleman here prepared to maintain that we are not *equal in the Union* according to the Constitution? If so, then I shall be able to understand his argument against the African Slave-trade, and in favor of the constitutionality of these enactments. * * * If it is right to buy slaves in Virginia, in what consists the wrong of buying slaves in Cuba, Brazil or upon the coast of Africa? * * * It is a law that *discriminates against Southern property;* no such discrimination is right. It is a law that discriminates against Southern labor: no such discrimination can be made *and our equality in the Union be not recognized.* I therefore invoke the principle of Free-trade here, the principle of State-rights, the principle of strict construction, and the *great fundamental principle of our right and equality in this Union,* and consequently of our right to erase from our statute-book every evidence of our *inequality,* that has been put there by the dominant and antagonistic class that has fed upon our very life-blood."

I might greatly multiply these extracts,—but I have given enough to show what you mean by the *principle* of State Equality, and for what purposes you demand the recognition of your absolute *right* to take your slaves, as your property, into the Territories. I do not suppose that the great mass of the Southern people hold these views of the principle, or join in demanding its recognition, with any such purpose. Neither did they dream in 1850 that the enactment of the Compromise measures contained a principle which would involve the repeal of the Missouri Compromise. But when they were told in 1854 that it did, they united in claiming the benefit of all the consequences of that principle, just as loudly as if they had been provided for at the outset. A man may have no thought of seizing his neighbor's farm ;—but show him that he has color of title, and he will speedily commence proceedings for its recovery. You and your associates in the organization and conduct of this movement know very well that, if you can establish the principle to-day, you can claim all the consequences that may flow from it to-morrow.

CAUSES OF THE DISUNION FEELING.

And this brings me to what I regard as the real motive of the disunion movement. That motive has taken precise and definite form, probably, in the minds of a comparatively small number of those who are most active in the movement itself. The great mass of those who sympathize with it and give it their aid, are governed by the vague but powerful feeling that the South, as a section, having peculiar institutions and peculiar necessities, *is gradually growing politically weaker and weaker in the* Union ;—that the North is rapidly gaining a preponderance in the Federal Councils ; and that there is no hope that the South can ever regain the ascendency, or even a political equality, under the Constitution and within the Union. The election of LINCOLN is regarded as conclusive proof that Northern supremacy is a fixed fact ; and it is on this account that it has so concentrated and intensified the resentment of the Southern States. No community ever sinks down willingly into a position of inferiority. Its instinct is to struggle against it, and the struggle will be violent in proportion to the magnitude of the evils which inferiority is believed to involve. All the sectional excitements and political paroxysms of the last twenty years, have been but the strenuous resistance of the South to what she has felt to be the inevitable tendency of events. The annexation of Texas,—the claim to California,—the repeal of the Missouri Compromise, —the fight for Kansas,—the fillibustering in Central America,—the clamor for Cuba, have been only the straws at which the slaveholding section has clutched, in the hope to save itself from being engulfed in the rising tide of Northern power. To them it was not the steady and silent rising of a peaceful sea. Its roar came to their ears upon the stormy blasts of Anti-Slavery fanaticism,—and sounded to them like the knell of destiny,—the precursor of degradation and ruin to their homes and their hopes.

I do not wonder at this alarm. I cannot blame it, or deny that it has its origin in just and patriotic sentiments. I do think that the leading intellects of the Southern States—those to whom as in

every community the great mass of the people look for guidance, and by whom they are guided, whether they know it or not,—ought to have foreseen this result and made up their minds long ago to act *with* the laws of Nature, rather than against them,—to yield to the spirit of the age, the tendencies of civilization and Christianity, instead of resisting them,—to make allies instead of enemies of those great moral principles which are proving too powerful for the mightiest monarchies of the earth, and before which it is idle to hope that despotism can make a permanent stand upon this continent. The Fathers of our Republic did so. They framed the Constitution upon such a basis, and in the belief that it would be administered in such a spirit. They gave the Government they created power over the Slave-trade,—not doubting that, after a few years, that power would be exercised with the general assent of all the States and that all would feel, as they felt, the necessity of providing for the gradual disappearance of Slavery itself. And for a series of years the event justified this expectation. The prohibition of the Slave-trade in 1807, recommended by JEFFERSON, was enacted with the unanimous consent of all the States North and South,—and down to 1830 there was a constant and hopeful tendency towards emancipation in nearly all the Slaveholding States. But since that time the leading intellects of the South have turned back the whole current of Southern sentiment upon this subject. In your own words, "an entirely new idea has sprung up, and is now universal in the South, upon the great question of Slavery, in its operation upon mankind and labor." Mr. CALHOUN taught the South that Slavery was, and must always be, the sole basis of its prosperity,—and that the leading aim of the South must be to fortify, to increase, and to make it perpetual. You and others have inherited his opinions, and devoted yourselves to their propagation. And in due process of time you have come into direct collision on this subject with the spirit and the letter of the Constitution which our Fathers framed ; and you now find that you cannot reach the object at which you aim, without destroying that Constitution, and breaking up the Union which it created.

The people of the South sympathize with the disunion movement from a keen sense of the growing superiority of the North. How that superiority can be overcome within the Union they do not perceive,—nor have they any definite idea of any policy by which it can be contested, after the South shall have seceded. You, on the contrary, have very definite ideas on both points. You trace the growing inequality of the two sections, in material development and consequent political power, *to the discrimination of the Federal Government against the South in regard to the supply of labor*,—which is in every community the great element of growth and of wealth. The North is permitted to increase indefinitely its supply of labor by immigration,—by inviting labor from abroad,—while the South is forbidden to seek a similar increase by importations of the peculiar kind of labor on which, most unwisely, it has come entirely to rely. When the price of labor rises in the North it invites and secures an additional supply from abroad;—and when the supply is excessive, it overflows into the new Territories, and, planting there new and free States, swells the political power of the North. At the South the enactments of Congress have arrested this natural operation of the law of supply and demand. When the price of labor rises at the South, there is no such resource for increasing the supply;—there is no way of lowering the price, and of securing a surplus to send into the new Territories. And this is the reason, in your opinion, why the South falls behind the North in material development and in political power. These laws forbidding the Slave-trade operate upon the South precisely as laws forbidding emigration would operate upon the North. *And the remedy you propose, is to be sought in the repeal of those laws.*—in permitting every State to import such labor as it requires. Then, as you say :

"The whole matter will be left to the operation of the law of supply and demand, precisely as the mule, the horse, the corn and the cotton trade are governed now, and I insist that *there should be no more discrimination by law against the Slave-trade than against the Nutmeg-trade of New-England. Let it be governed by the law of supply and demand alone.* If we do not want the negroes, then we do not have them ; if we do want them, then we can get them. I think this ought to be governed by that rule."

This, then, is your ground of discontent with the Federal Government,—that it *prevents the increase of Slavery.* And I believe it to be at the root of the disunion feeling now so prevalent in the cotton-growing States. Probably not one in ten of the mass of the Southern people,—perhaps not one in five of those who are to-day in favor of secession,—would declare themselves in favor of reopening the Slave-trade. Nor is it your policy to press the subject upon their attention, or even to allow it to be made a topic of discussion, while the issue of secession is pending. You have made up your mind that your object cannot be attained within the Union. "I do not expect," you said at Montgomery, "that the North, which has the majority, will ever vote for the measure,—

therefore *these laws will never be repealed."* You are therefore for secession. But it would not be safe to trust the issue, either before or after that event, to the general action of all the Slaveholding States,—for several of them are known to be utterly hostile to it. As you declared at Montgomery, it is the interest of Virginia to have negroes scarce, because they will command a high price,—while it is for the interest of Georgia, South Carolina, and Alabama to have them numerous, in order to have them cheap. You, propose, therefore, to exclude the Frontier States from all consultation upon this subject,—and from all agency in the formation of the new Confederacy which you propose to establish. "Virginia and the other Frontier States," says the Charleston *Mercury,* the organ and mouthpiece of your party. "may as well at once understand their position with the Cotton States. *The Southern States will disregard their counsel.* They intend to secede from the Union, and construct a Union *among themselves,* and will be glad to find Virginia and other Border States in counsel with them *after this great revolution."* And other journals in the disunion interest, deprecate the discussion of the Slave-trade issue as certain to divide public sentiment, and weaken, if not destroy, the entire secession movement.

At present it is your policy to accumulate arguments for disunion, rather than to sift and define them. You can command far more support for that measure by declaiming on the growing power and preponderance of the North, and the steadily waning influence of the South in the federal councils, than by tracing them to their cause and fixing public attention upon the remedy you propose to apply. But the time will come when specific measures must be proposed,—and then foremost among them will be the restoration of the African Slave-trade.

I think you are quite right in believing that the Federal Government will never consent to the reopening of that traffic. The North will never concede that point,—nor lay the foundation for its concession,—directly or indirectly, under any circumstances, nor for any consideration which you can offer as an equivalent. They will meet you on this issue upon any field you may select. They will accept the hazard of Disunion a thousand times, rather than that as its alternative.

III.

SECESSION UNCONSTITUTIONAL, AND IMPOSSIBLE WITHOUT WAR.

New-York, Dec. 10, 1860.

You will see from my last letter that I have no faith in the validity or sincerity of the reasons assigned for a secession of the Southern States. The motive for that movement is neither the failure of the North to surrender fugitive slaves, nor the enactment of Personal Liberty bills, nor the practical inability of Southern slaveholders to take their slaves into the Territories of the United States. If you could have full and sufficient guarantees upon every one of these points you would be just as zealous, though not perhaps so sanguine, an advocate of secession as you are now. What you and your associate conspirators seek is the restoration of the African Slave-trade. To use your own words, " We of Alabama *want slaves to be cheap ;*—we want to buy, not to sell them. It is a Virginia idea that slaves ought to be high. Virginia wants $1,500 each for her negroes :—*we want to get them cheaper.*" " CHEAP NEGROES " is the grand consummation at which you aim,—the mighty motive which rouses you to the task of destroying a Government which was formed to " secure the blessings of Liberty to ourselves and our posterity."

You will not understand me as implying that this is the motive of all whom you have enlisted in the secession movement. If it were, you would not persist so vehemently in excluding all but the Cotton States from your counsels. You would have admitted Virginia and Tennessee and Kentucky to a share in the conduct of your conspiracy. If this were a movement in the interest of all the Slaveholding States, it would have been decided in a general convention of them all. But you know very well that in such a convention it would be impossible to conceal your real motive,—and that its exposure would be fatal to the scheme. Virginia is now, as she has been from the earliest moment of her independent existence, opposed to the Slave-trade :—South Carolina, therefore, gives her formal notice that her aid is not desired, and that her advice will not be heeded, in the movement of secession. Kentucky, Tennessee, Maryland—all the {Frontier States would set their faces like a flint against reopening the African Slave-trade. They are to have no voice, therefore, in the decision of the question : it is only after the Revolution shall have been accomplished that they will be " permitted " to join your new Confederacy. Even in South Carolina you deprecate a discussion of the subject. For you know that the more intelligent and considerate portion of the people, even in the Gulf States, are opposed to this cardinal feature of your policy. They believe, as we do, that we have negroes enough on this Continent already. They know that whatever may be their relations to society,— whether slave or free,—they are a draw-back upon

our civilization,—a clog upon the refinement and Christian culture of the community into which they are thrust.

This subject, therefore, is to be kept out of sight until disunion shall have been accomplished. The great mass of the people in the Slaveholding States are to be moved by other considerations. Their pride, their local jealousies, their fears, have been practiced upon by way of preparation for the " proper moment," when they are to be precipitated into revolution. Once out of the Union, their destinies will be in the hands of the boldest and the strongest of their leaders. The Gulf States are first to organize the new Government,—and determine the fundamental basis on which it shall rest. Absolute free trade in " negroes from Africa as in mules from Malta," will be the corner-stone of this new temple. Each State will be permitted to trade in whatever it may prefer,—to import negroes or nutmegs, at its own discretion. And the Frontier States will be offered this alternative,— either to join the new Confederacy upon these terms,—to join the North, with the certainty of being compelled to emancipate their slaves, or to stand between the two, and receive the blows and the buffetings of both.

It is by no means impossible that this ingenious, double conspiracy, against the Union and the frontier Slave States, may meet with at least a partial and temporary success. But even if you should establish an independent Confederation or consolidation of the Cotton States, can you suppose for a moment that you would be permitted by the civilized nations of the world to reopen the African Slave-trade and efface the brand which all Christendom has combined to fix upon it ? All the great Powers of the earth have entered into treaties, or have made laws, by which that trade is declared to be piracy, and have pledged their united strength for its extinction. Do you expect them to abrogate these treaties at the demand of your Southern Confederacy ? Do you expect them to relax their vigilance in enforcing them ? By what inducements would you bring about such a result ? Part of your scheme is to extend your conquests into Mexico and Central America,—to add control of the Caribbean Sea to your supremacy over the Gulf,—to bring Cuba into your Southern Union. Are these designs likely to meet the views and enlist the sympathies of either England or France ? You rely perhaps, on the favor with which the Apprenticeship system has been regarded by France, and the indications that it may be tolerated even by England. But you must remember that these measures are resorted to only for the supply of their own necessities, not for the building up of rival States, and that the principle has been insisted on by both nations, as indispensable, that the emigration shall be voluntary,—that the service stipulated shall be for a term of years and be paid for, and that the most perfect security shall be given for a full compliance with these conditions, and for discharging and returning the laborers at the expiration of the stipulated term. Even in this form,it is by no means certain that England and France will enter upon the system. But would such a system answer your purposes ? You want *slaves*—not appren-. tices—slaves for life,—who shall be property, not persons,—incapable of consent or stipulation of any kind,—who shall have no rights which white men will be bound to respect,—with whom no bargain is binding, and whose children and children's children, shall thus be mere property, absolutely and to the remotest generation. Anything short of this, any limitations or conditions upon the traffic, would introduce into the system of Slavery as it now exists among you, elements fatal to its continuance. You must be strangely insensible to the moral sentiment of the age,—to the ideas which are steadily advancing to supremacy over the Christian world,—if you expect ever to gain the assent of any civilized nation on the face of the earth to such a scheme.

The first result of successful secession would be to increase immensely the vigor and vigilance of the great naval Powers in suppressing the Slave-trade. Nothing has paralyzed those efforts hitherto half so much as the unwillingness of our Federal Government to offend the South by any special zeal in this direction. It has been made, to some extent, an American question, and has been complicated by considerations of naval rights and of national honor. Our refusal to concede a mutual right of search, and the hesitation of England to enforce upon Spain the fulfillment of her treaty stipulations, lest she should become involved in a war which might end in the transfer of Cuba to the United States, have done more than all other causes combined to prevent or embarrass the suppression of the Slave-trade. Both these obstacles would be removed by secession. The North will have no motive for further hesitation. The mutual right of search will be conceded. The Slave-trade, if prosecuted at all, will be prosecuted just as piracy is, —under the ban and outlawry of the world. The moral sentiment of this country will be released from the shackles which the Constitution, and the Union with the slaveholding South have imposed upon it, and the Slave-trade will lose the only shadow of toleration it has hitherto enjoyed.

Even if you secede, therefore, and establish your new Slave Empire, you will be 'no nearer the object you seek than you are at present.

THE QUESTION OF SECESSION.

And now let us consider this subject of secession. What is it ? On what basis does it rest ? Under what form, and by what means, do you propose to achieve it ?

In the first place, you claim that Secession is a constitutional right—that this Confederacy being the result of a compact between sovereign States, each State has a right to withdraw from it at pleasure.

When a State, therefore, declares itself out of the Union, the Federal Government has no right to coerce it into remaining. It has no power to make war on a State. The President of the United States holds this opinion—that is, he comes as near as holding it as he does to holding any opinion on this subject.

Now, I do not propose to discuss the question whether the Constitution is or is not a "compact." That may be an important point to settle, but it seems to me quite immaterial to the present issue. For even if it is a compact, and nothing more, I can see no reason why one of the thirty-two parties to it should have the right to break it at discretion. A compact implies a mutual obligation. It is binding upon all who become parties to it. It is so alike in private and in public transactions. If two men form a partnership, unlimited in its term, that partnership can only be dissolved by mutual consent, or by appeal to a common arbiter. In the lowest form of private compacts, no one party to a bargain has the right to repudiate it at pleasure,—to absolve himself from the obligations and responsibilities which it involves, and resume the position which he held before he entered into it. Nor can States or nations claim any exemption from this law of common morals. Nothing is more firmly established in the laws of nations and the usages of the world than the principle that a deliberate repudiation of treaty obligations is a just cause of war. Even if the Union, then, be only a treaty,—a compact between the States,—it is nevertheless binding upon them all. Each one is bound to abide by all its engagements, —to discharge faithfully the obligations into which it has entered.

You may say they are sovereign, and, therefore, sole masters of their own acts,—judges of their own obligations,—and subject to no common and controlling tribunal. Even if they were so once, they ceased to be so when they parted with a portion of their sovereignty and agreed to accept a common arbiter. No nation can be so absolutely sovereign as not to be bound by its own obligations.

Suppose we take the opposite position,—that any State has a right to secede at will : where will it land us ? If one State may secede another may. Suppose all resolve upon secession : What becomes of the Federal Government ? What becomes of its obligations,—of its debts,—its common property,— of its engagements entered into with foreign Powers ? What becomes of its flag, its army, its navy ? All these things, you say, are to be matters of future arrangement. But that does not settle the question of legality. If secession is a matter of constitutional right,—then there must be some constitutional provision, direct or inferential, for the emergencies which grow out of it. All these obligations are to be annulled ;—but then, you say, they may be renewed if the thirty-two parties to the old compact see fit to renew them. But what if they do not ? What would foreign creditors of the United States say to such a scheme ? What would foreign nations say to such a mode of disposing of the engagements and undertakings into which they have entered with the Republic?

THE GOVERNMENT DEALS WITH INDIVIDUALS, AND NOT WITH STATES.

But it seems to me that this question has been involved in a great deal of needless confusion, by the use of the term *secession*. "Words are things," and in this instance, as in many others, the adroit substitution of one word for another has created an issue entirely foreign to the case. The Federal Government is under no necessity of discussing the question of secession. The only point it has to decide is *the right and the duty of enforcing obedience to its own laws.*

The Constitution gives Congress power to make certain laws for the people of the United States. It is the duty of every citizen of the United States to obey those laws, provided they are constitutional, and to refer that point to tribunals created for the purpose of deciding it. Has the Federal Government the right and the power to enforce such obedience upon its citizens? No one can doubt it. You do not deny it. The Government has used the Army and the Navy to enforce the Fugitive Slave law in Massachusetts, and you have never denied or questioned the constitutionality of that proceeding. It has precisely the same right to use the Army and the Navy to enforce upon a citizen of South Carolina the payment of duties which Congress may impose upon the importation of merchandize abroad. The *State* has nothing to do with the matter. The law does not take effect upon the State; the Constitution does not even recognize the existence of the State, in connection with the duty of obedience to the laws of Congress, except to forbid its effective interference. The only way in which the State can be brought into the case at all, is by claiming the right to release its citizens from the duty of obedience to the Federal law. Congress says that the citizen of South Carolina shall pay duties upon all merchandise he may import into Charleston. The State of South Carolina assumes that she has a Constitutional right to release him from that obligation—and to say that he may import that merchandise *without* paying duties. The only question that can arise is has South Carolina any such right? Let the Constitution itself reply:

" This Constitution and the *laws of the United States*, which shall be made in pursuance thereof; and all treaties made, or which shall be made, under the authority of the United States, *shall be the supreme law of the land*, and the judges in every State *shall be bound thereby*, ANYTHING IN THE CONSTITUTION OR LAWS OF ANY STATE TO THE CONTRARY NOTWITHSTANDING."

This is the whole case. There is no question of coercing a State—or of "making war" on a State. The laws of Congress are not made for States—but for individuals All that is required of the States is that they shall not release their citizens from the duty of obedience. Indeed, they cannot do so. South Carolina may declare herself out of the Union twice a year, if she pleases,—and pass as many nullification laws as her statute-books will hold ; but she cannot impair in the slightest degree the duty of every individual within her borders to obey the laws of Congress. It is the duty of the President of the United States to " take care that the laws be faithfully executed ;" and, as Mr. BUCHANAN very justly remarks in his Message, " no human power can release him from the performance of that duty."

THE STATES HAVE NO POWER TO RELEASE THEIR CITIZENS FROM THE DUTY OF OBEDIENCE.

The only question which can arise, therefore, in this matter of secession is, whether the Federal Government will permit citizens of South Carolina or Alabama, or any other State, to refuse obedience to the laws of Congress on the plea that they have been released from such obedience by the action of that State. So far as the matter of right is concerned, the question scarcely requires an answer. Unless we have made up our minds to abandon our national existence altogether, we have no choice in the premises. For if the principle is once conceded that a State may nullify the action of the Federal Government, and release is citizens from the duty of obedience to Federal law, neither South Carolina nor the Slave States will be left alone in the exercise of that right. Every Northern and Western State will at once enact Personal Liberty bills of the most stringent character. New-York has a hundred fold more to gain by releasing her citizens from the payment of Federal duties on imports than any Southern State.

But you urge that ours is a voluntary Government,—and must depend on the voluntary assent of its people, and not on force, for its preservation. Properly understood, this is perfectly true,—but its practical importance depends on the manner of its application. If a constitutional majority of the people become dissatisfied with the Government, or with its Administration, they have a right to change it. If any considerable portion of the people become dissatisfied, they have a right to demand amendments. If they consider themselves aggrieved or oppressed, they may seek redress in the Courts of law. And back of all these rights is the right of Revolution, for which no provision can ever be made—which, indeed, can never be recognized in any Constitution or form of Government, because it is simply the right of appealing to force against a Government which is found to be hopelessly oppressive. But our Government is not a voluntary government in any such sense as that individual citizens are left to their voluntary choice whether to obey the laws or not,—or that communities, large or small, organized or unorganized, have a constitutional right to repudiate the obligations of the Constitution. Such a government would be no government at all. It would have none of the functions, none of the powers, none of the stability which are inseparable from the very idea of government. All government implies force,—the right of coercion. And the consent on which our Government rests is the voluntary concent of the people that force may be used, if necessary, to constrain obedience to law.

I concede fully that as the laws depend for their vitality and practical validity upon the co-operation of the governed, they should never outrage the principles, the interests or the sentiments of the people among whom they are to be enforced. A disregard of this principle, might, under aggravated circumstances, and in default of all other redress, justify revolution,—a local protest in arms against the execution of the obnoxious law. It is by overlooking entirely this principle that the Fugitive Slave law has been rendered at once so odious and so inoperative. A law of Congress guaranteeing freedom of speech on Slavery to a Northern Abolitionist, in the heart of a Slaveholding State, though it might be strictly constitutional, would be not only ineffective, but would rouse the most bitter hostility of the community whose safety it would seriously endanger.

But you will urge that this doctrine converts the Federal Government into a consolidated despotism. Not so,—for this Federal sovereignty extends only to those matters which are expressly delegated to it. It is restricted by the Constitution which creates it and prescribes the scope of its activity. But up to the limit of those restrictions the sovereignty of the Federal Government is just as complete as is that of the States over all the matters which are reserved. You say this sovereignty was delegated by the States themselve, and may, therefore, be resumed. On the contrary, even if that were true, the fact that it was delegated proves that it *cannot* be resumed. Its derivation cannot alter its character or impair its force. If the States gave it, they parted with what they gave,and they cannot recall the gift. They clothed the Federal Government with power to make laws, on certain subjects, which should be of binding obligation upon the individual inhabitants of the United States—and with the right to enforce obedience to those laws by the armed power of the country, if that should be necessary. So far were they from reserving to themselves as States the right of releasing their citizens from the duty of obedience, that they required all their State officers, Governors, legislators and judges, to take a solemn oath that they would enforce those laws, and they stipulated moreover that nothing in the Constitution or laws of any State should derogate in any degree from the absolute supremacy of the laws of Congress. Those laws, according to the "compact," even if the Constitution be nothing more, are to be the "supreme law of the land, anything in the Constitution or laws of any State to the contrary notwithstanding."

Any claim, therefore, on the part of a State of a constitutional right to release its citizens from the duty of obeying the laws of Congress, made in pursuance of the Constitution, is simply preposterous and absurd.

Any exercise of such an asserted right—any attempt to prevent the Federal Government from executing those laws by State legislation, is merely a nullity. Alabama, Georgia and South Carolina, may pass as many laws as they please forbidding their citizens to pay duties to the Federal Government, to obey process of Federal Courts, or to regard the Federal law prohibiting the Slave-trade. Every one of them will be null and void. Must the Federal Government, then, you may ask, "*make war*" on Alabama or South Carolina for enacting such laws? Not at all,—simply because it is needless, the laws being themselves a nullity, and because, moreover, the Federal Government has nothing to do with States as such. It has no right to say what bills they shall pass and what they shall not. It deals with individuals,—and requires *them* to obey its laws. If they refuse, it may compel obedience. If the State interposes, and resists such attempted compulsion,—then *the State "makes war" upon the Federal Government*,—not a war that can be recognized as such by independent Powers,—because it is not a war between such Powers,—but a war of rebellion,—a war of revolution. And the only question that remains is, whether the Federal Government has a right to put down rebellion,—to suppress insurrection against its authority. And that question seems to me equivalent to asking whether it is a Government at all, or only a sham,—a pretence of Government, without any of its real powers or faculties.

I have no doubt, therefore, that the Federal Government has the right, under the Constitution, to do what you would style "compelling a State to remain in the Union,"—that is, to compel every citizen within the jurisdiction of the United States to obey the laws of Congress. Nor have I the slightest hesitation in saying that it is its duty to do so,—and that any President, Senator, or Member of Congress who refuses to aid, in doing so, violates his oath of office, and makes himself an aider and abettor of treason and rebellion. As to the *mode* and *time* of compulsion,—the means of bringing stress to bear upon rebellious communities, and the measure of force to be used,—these are very different questions, to be decided on other grounds and by the wise discretion of the Federal Government. That Government may deem it most expedient, because most likely to prove effective, to postpone all resort to force to the latest possible moment,—to abstain from all appearance of coercion,—and to trust to the moral compulsion of time, of reflection and experience, rather than a hasty resort to material power. But it cannot surrender the *right*. It cannot acknowledge the power of any State to release its citizens from the duty of obedience to the Constitution and the laws of the United States. Such an acknowledgment would be simply an overthrow of the Constitution.

IMPOSSIBILITY OF PEACEABLE SECESSION.

South Carolina is on the eve of "withdrawing from the Union,"—as she phrases it,—that is, of enacting State laws releasing her citizens from the duty of obeying the laws of Congress, organizing herself into an independent sovereignty and preparing to resist, by force of arms, any attempt of the present Government to enforce obedience to its laws upon her citizens. Her first attempt,—as it will be her first necessity,—will be to *obtain a recognition of her independence from the Federal Government*. Have you the slightest idea that she will succeed? The President has no power to grant such a recognition. Congress has no power under the Constitution to grant it. Where is such recognition to come from? Clearly it can only come from the people of the United States,—meeting in Convention as they met in 1767 for the purpose of dissolving one Confederacy and substituting another in its place. We must go through precisely the same process as our Fathers did when they abrogated the old Confederation, and created the " more perfect Union," which during the seventy years of its existence has given us more peace, prosperity and national greatness than have ever been achieved by any other nation on the face of the earth. We are now called upon to destroy that Union. Why? Because it has failed to "provide for the common defence, promote the general welfare, and secure the blessings of liberty to ourselves and our posterity?" No: but because it has *not* failed. Because it does not permit the continuance of the African Slave-trade:—because it does not recognize slaves as "property,"—to be guaranteed to their owners wherever its jurisdiction may extend:—because its tendencies are not towards strengthening Slavery and making it perpetual and permanent in the Federal Government, but rather the other way. You cannot expect the People of the United States to consent to abolish the Union and repeal the Constitution for such reasons as these. And yet that is what they must do, if they recognize the independence of South Carolina.

If South Carolina could be dealt with singly in this matter,—if she could be released alone from the Union without conceding principles which would release every State from its allegiance, abolish the Constitution, and blot out the Republic from its place among the nations, there would be very little difficulty in adjusting the matter. She would go out of the Union with the unanimous consent of the other States. One of her own writers, in the *Southern Quarterly Review*, has asserted that a majority of her inhabitants were Tories in the Revolution, and were opposed to independence. Their descendants have inherited their political sentiments. South Carolina has never had a particle of sympathy with the fundamental principles which lie at the basis of our Republican institutions. From the very outset she has been at war with the dominant ideas of the Confederacy. She has done more to embroil the country in controversy, to disturb the public peace and sow the seeds of disloyalty and strife than all the other States. And if there were any warrant in the Constitution for secession I should favor the immediate secession of all the other States from any confederacy in which she might have a place. But this cannot be done. Nor can we ignore the fact that she does not intend to go out alone. We are asked to permit her withdrawal merely as preliminary to that of all the Cotton, possibly of all the Slaveholding, States.

What we have to decide, therefore, when we are asked to recognize the independence of South Carolina, is, whether we will consent to the disruption of our Union for the sake of creating a Southern Confederacy,—or rather a Military Despotism, resting possibly on Democratic forms like that of France, (for that is the shape your new government would probably take,) upon our Southern border. You and your confederates in disunion seem to think we would. You must base such a sentiment upon a serious over-estimate of our disinterestedness and good nature, or upon an equally serious under-estimate of our intelligence and good sense.

DISUNION MEANS WAR.

I put aside for the present all considerations connected with the character of your proposed Government,—the fact that Slavery is to be the basis of its existence, and the interest of Slavery the paramount aim of its policy. Setting aside the certainties of constant contentions and wars between two great nations thus widely separated in principle, in feeling and purpose, and by no material barriers to keep them apart,—look at the position in which we should be placing ourselves with reference to the future. We should be surrendering to a foreign and a hostile power more than half of the Atlantic seaboard,—the whole Gulf,—the mouth of the Mississippi, with its access to the open sea, and its drainage of the commerce of the mighty West,—all the feasible Railroad routes to the Pacific,—all chance of further accessions from Mexico, Central America or the West India islands,—and all prospect of ever extending our growth and national development in the only direction in which such extension will ever be possible. We should be limiting ourselves to that narrow belt of the continent which would be bounded by the British Colonies on the north, the Slave Empire on the south, and the Rocky Mountains on the west. Have you seen any indications which encourage the hope of so magnificent a self-sacrifice on the part of our people? What is there in our past history to lead you to consider us thus reckless of national growth and national grandeur? Is it the millions we have expended in the purchase of Florida, and Louisiana, and Texas? Is it the hundreds of millions we expended in a war with Mexico for the conquest of Texas and California? Is it the seven millions we paid for the Messilla Valley and the acquisition of feasible Railroad routes to the Pacific Ocean? We have a few men among us, dreamers rather than statesmen, who would cast all these considerations aside and accept any degree of national humiliation in order to rid their consciences of what they regard as their "responsibility for the sin of Slavery." But they are very few and very powerless. Nine-tenths of our people in the Northern and Northwestern States would wage a war longer than the war of Independence before they will assent to any such surrender of their aspirations and their hopes. There is no nation in the world so ambitious of growth and of power,—so thoroughly pervaded with the spirit of conquest, —so filled with dreams of enlarged dominion, as ours. In New-England these impulses have lost something of their natural force under the influences of culture and the peaceful arts. But in the Centre and the West, this thirst for national power still rages unrestrained.

To this consideration are to be added others of still greater weight with other classes of our community. Your Southern Empire, resting upon Slavery as its basis, must be conformed more and more to the spirit and the forms which Slavery requires. A standing army will be your first necessity, and the rigor with which your slave population are kept in subjection, must increase from year to year. You will have less and less of education,—more and more of brute force,—and your slaves will sink lower and lower in the scale of creation with every succeeding year. You know enough of Northern character to estimate the effect which this would have upon the minds of the conscientious portion of our Northern people, and how thoroughly it would alienate them from their new neighbors. You could not count upon their forbearance or their sympathy in the slightest degree. Every little misunderstanding that might arise would swell the hostility of the two peoples, and bring them into inevitable and deadly collision

Even, therefore, if at the outset the impulses of our people should prompt an assent to your secession, it could not be permanent. Just now the feeling of the North seems to be in favor of letting you go. This is the first prompting of the genuine kindness that pervades the popular heart,—an indisposition to do injury to any section,—a hope that both may go along peacefully and prosperously without collision or strife of any kind. But a very little reflection will show the futility of such expectations. The thing is impossible. The only condition of our remaining at peace is that we remain one. Disunion means War,—a war of conquest,—a war of subjugation on the one side or the other. You may say it would be hopeless to attempt to subjugate the South. Possibly;—but this is a point which nations never take for granted in advance. It is not the conviction of the masses of our people. They believe the South to be comparatively weak, and this belief, whether just or not, will do all its mischief by leading to the beginning of war. What the end will be the future alone could show.

South Carolina must not expect, therefore, to be recognized by the Federal Government as an in-dependent State, *without a war.* Any such recognition by an Administration, as a mere legislative act, would be treason to the Constitution, and would justify a revolution. It can only be done through an amendment of the Constitution—by a formal dissolution of the nation, and the creation of another upon its ruins. To that the people, who constitute the nation, will never consent. You must win your independence, if you win it at all, just as every other nation has done—by the Sword.

NO AID FROM FOREIGN POWERS.

But you count upon the assistance of foreign Powers,—especially of France and England. This seems to me the wildest dream that ever misled the minds of desperate or over-sanguine conspirators. How has LOUIS NAPOLEON kept his Imperial throne,—but by taking his people into alliance with him—by representing in his person and policy their sentiments, their ideas, their passion especially for making themselves the champions of freedom in other lands? The French idea of liberty is freedom to make others free. The Italian war was popular because it was a war to liberate the enslaved Italians. The first indication of a possible desertion of that cause, and an alliance with the Princes who had oppressed them, shook the Imperial throne. How long would he hold that throne if he were to wage a war in support of Austria, either in Italy or in Hungary? Now, any interference of France on your behalf would be an interference on behalf of Slavery. And these same considerations are still stronger when applied to England. The people of England are fanatical in their hatred of negro Slavery. And no Ministry that should give the slightest hint of favor to a movement for Slavery in any form could hold its place a week

Nor can you presume at all upon the hatred of free institutions which prevails among the Governments of Europe. That hatred does not pervade the people, nor can it, therefore, to any considerable extent, influence the action of the Governments, especially of England and France, where the popular will has controlling weight. England's dominant purpose just now, moreover, is to secure the alliance of the United States, in preparation for the great struggle between free and absolute Governments, which she thinks is impending. Besides all this, the great interest of both England and France, so far as this country is concerned, is *commerce.* Whatever promotes their trade with us brings them all the advantage they can ever expect to reap from their relations with us. And whatever promotes our prosperity and our ability to sell and buy, builds up that trade. Neither of these countries has the slightest interest in our disunion, or in any differences which shall retard our growth. They may deprecate the imitation of our example in their own countries. They may declaim against us, and point out our weaknesses and faults to prevent their own people from introducing universal suffrage, the vote by ballot, and annual Parliaments. But they have no wish for our downfall, as they have no interest in it. Neither of them could sustain any heavier blow than the destruction of our commerce would involve.

Nor will either of them recognize the independence of any seceding Southern State until that independence shall have become an established fact, by the recognition of our own Government, or by such demonstration of its ability to maintain it by force of arms as shall leave no room for doubt. Precisely the same course will be pursued in this case as was pursued in that of Texas,—and as is pursued in every case under similar circumstances. Any attempt on the part of any foreign Power to aid in the rebellion of a Southern State, would be an act of open and flagrant hostility to the Government of the United States, and would be resented as such. Whatever might be the disposition of our Government towards secession, we should never permit a foreign Power to interfere in a matter so purely of domestic concern.

If you enter upon this matter of secession, you must enter upon it alone. You will have no help from any foreign Power—neither troops, nor ships, nor arms. You cannot borrow money anywhere, because you have nothing whatever to pledge for its security. You have neither credit nor the means of gaining credit abroad. The only one of the slaveholding States which has ever tried the faith of foreign creditors to any extent, has, by her shameless repudiation—her steady breach of faith—branded the whole section to which she belongs with the ineffaceable marks of disgrace and distrust;—and the example of Mississippi will be a perpetual warning to every capitalist in Europe against lending a dollar to any Southern State. You cannot call upon your own people for supplies, for their sole wealth consists in negroes and lands, which, in case of war, will fall to a tithe of their present value. Nor can you conceal from yourselves any more than from the rest of the world the dreadful danger you would incur, of an insurrection of slaves from one end of the South to the other, the moment they shall see you engaged in a war against States which are seeking, as you have taught them to believe, to effect their emancipation. All these accumulated horrors you must face alone,—relying upon your own resources. without a word or a thought of sympathy from any nation on earth,—under the frown of all Christendom,—with the settled conviction in the breasts of half your own people that you are fighting against every impulse of humanity, every tendency of the Christian civilization of the age which shall witness this strange, this horrible contention!

THE COTTON ARGUMENT.

You rely on COTTON to save you from all this. "The world must have our Cotton," you say. " England must have it or her looms will stop—her workmen will be thrown out of employment—riots, starvation and civil war will desolate her realm. She will open our ports, if the Federal Government shall persist in closing them." If you rely upon such a hope to sustain you through the dread ordeal of revolution, you are destined to a rude disenchantment. You can no more prevent either England or the North from procuring your Cotton, if you find leisure from war to raise it, than you can prevent water from running to the sea. The laws which regulate the currents of trade are just as fixed and unchangeable as the laws which govern matter. We may not understand them so thoroughly, but we know enough of them to know that we can no more withstand or change their operation than we can that of the laws of gravity. Of what avail were the Berlin and Milan decrees, though backed by a million men in arms? Upon whom fell the weight of the old embargo which you are threatening to renew?

You may make as many laws as you please,—you can never prevent your cotton from finding its way to the market where it commands the highest price,—and if you could, your own people would be the first to perish under the operation. For why do you raise cotton but to sell it? You can neither eat it, nor drink it,—nor feed your slaves with it,—nor wear it until you have sent it abroad or to the North to be manufactured. Even now you buy from the North every year a hundred and fifty millions of dollars worth of food and utensils of labor and other necessaries of life,—which you must have, and which you cannot get unless you pay for them with your only great product,—your sole reliance,—the cotton which you raise. You could distress England if you could withhold your cotton—but it would be at the cost of starvation and ruin at home. The manufacture of cotton is but one branch of British industry : but the selling of cotton is the only reliance of the Southern States. Blot that out, and you blot out the prosperity and even the existence of Southern industry. You not only ruin the planter, and drive his slaves to starvation or insurrection,—but you kill the business of every Southern Railroad, the traffic of every Southern river, the labor of every Southern City. In such a contest of physical and financial endurance, which would hold out longest, England or the Southern States? Which would repent soonest, the English mill-owner or the Southern planter?

You expect to invite the ships of the world to your ports by making them free. This is your main reliance for ruining the commerce of the North and turning its wealth into your own channels. You must remember, in the first place. that you can have no free-trade until you have achieved your independence. But waiving that obstacle for the moment, you must know that such a policy on your part would be met, whenever it should become necessary to meet it at all, by a corresponding policy on ours. Charleston, Baltimore, Savannah and New-Orleans could not be free ports many months before Boston, New-York and Philadelphia would be free ports also. With the advantages we should have at the outset,—our enormous mercantile marine our trained and hardy sailors, our skill in ship-building, and our capital already invested in commerce, can you doubt the result of such an unequal race? You rely on the manufactories of New-England and Pennsylvania to prevent such a result. And even so sensible a man as Mr. STEPHENS predicts universal anarchy at the North as the effect of disunion. He has much to learn of the temper and spirit of the North if he anticipates any such result. Undoubtedly great interests in both these sections would suffer serious injury from the adoption of a free-trade policy ; but other interests would gain just as much, and the versatility of our people is so great that they would very speedily adapt themselves to the changed necessities of the case. If New-York were a free port her commerce would be doubled in ten years. In spite of everything the South could do,—in spite of tariffs, attempted prohibitions and bounties upon commerce, the North, through her manufactures, or her commerce, would supply, as she does now, every plantation in every Southern State with every article of luxury which would be needed from abroad.

I pass over in this place all considerations of the domestic difficulties you would encounter in your enterprise,—your differences as to the form of government to be established ;—the clashing of interests between the several sections of your own Confederacy ;—the heavy direct taxation by which, under a free trade policy, all the expenses of your Government must be met ;—the fundamental and fatal question on what kinds of property and in what proportions that tax should be levied ;—your exposure to the hostility of the whole civilized world, and the impossibility of your raising a Navy wherewith to meet it ;—all these and many other practical difficulties, which would obstruct your progress at every step, may safely be dismissed in the present discussion, with this bare reference to them.

Those, then, are the reasons which lead me to believe that you will not succeed in your enterprise of destroying this Union and erecting a new Slaveholding and Slave-trading Empire on its ruins. I have still to consider the Duty of the North and the true Policy of the South in the political crisis which you have brought upon the country. But that I must reserve for a concluding letter.

IV.

THE PRECISE NATURE OF THE PENDING ISSUE—THE DUTY OF THE NORTH AND THE TRUE POLICY OF THE SLAVEHOLDING STATES.

NEW-YORK, Tuesday, Dec. 25, 1860.

Hon. W. L. YANCEY—*Sir :* In my last letter I gave you my reasons for regarding Secession as simply Revolution, and for believing that it can neither be peaceful nor successful. I propose now to state my understanding of the nature of the contest, and my reasons for hoping that it will not be compromised nor postponed,—but finally *settled,* by whatever process and through whatever tribulations may be necessary.

I do not mean to say that I am opposed to measures of conciliation in the present crisis. I am not. I regard the present excitement at the South as artificial—or, at least, as feverish and unnatural. It has been produced by temporary stimulants, and unfits the Southern people from making and meeting the real issue on its merits. You and your confederates have filled the Southern mind with the most perilous misrepresentations concerning the Republican Party. You have taught them to regard it as an Abolition Party,—and have assured them that its advent to power would be the signal for a violent crusade against the rights of the Southern States and the peace of Southern society. The past five years have been devoted, with the utmost zeal and assiduity, by all the leading politicians of the South, to the inculcation of this fearful falsehood. Men of all parties there have joined in it,—not because

they believed it, but because they had objects of political or personal ambition which could not be accomplished without it. They have done their work thoroughly and effectually. The whole Southern mind is pervaded with this baseless belief. On every plantation,—by every fireside,—in every negro hut, the general talk is of coming emancipation. LINCOLN and the Republicans are talked about at the South as if they were a horde of black and bloodthirsty savages,—eager to feast on Southern sorrows, and to plunge Southern society into anarchy and insurrection. You have closed the gates of the South against all efforts to correct these false impressions. No journal that protests against them is permitted to circulate among the mass of the Southern people. No man who knows their falsehood and their danger dare lift his voice to remonstrate. The delusion, fatal as it is false, is hugged to the Southern bosom as if it were the anchor of their hopes, and the only ground of their salvation.

The result of all this is an inflammation of the public mind, which renders all chance of rational treatment for the moment hopeless. The first thing to be done is to allay that inflammation,—to bring the South into a sane and healthy mood,—to prevent her, if possible, from inflicting upon herself some rash and insane blow while the access of the fever is on, and thus obtain time and opportunity for a more sensible and radical treatment of the case. And for this purpose I am willing to resort to any emollients that may be useful. But, as the Republican Party has no power, as yet, to *act* in the premises,—as its foes, your confederates, are still entrenched in the citadel of Federal power, all we can do is to use the language of conciliation and make verbal protest against the fundamental falsehood which is working all this wrong.

But this is only a temporary and preliminary process. It leaves the real difference unadjusted ; and this the interest of the whole country forbids. We have reached a point in our political history when the welfare of both North and South requires that we should understand distinctly the basis on which our Government rests—the spirit which is to guide its administration,—the *relations it is to hold to the institution of Slavery.* The election of Mr. LINCOLN marks an era in the political history of the country,—and his Administration is to decide the issue and bring the conflict to a close.

SENTIMENTS AND POLICY OF THE FRAMERS OF THE CONSTITUTION CONCERNING SLAVERY.

No unprejudiced person can study the history of the formation of the Constitution of the United States without perceiving, that the founders of the Republic had certain clear opinions concerning Slavery, and, in spite of its inherent difficulties and embarrassments, a distinct and definite policy in regard to it. Those opinions were expressed more or less fully in their public debates, and in their private correspondence, to which in part the lapse of time has given us access ; and their policy was embodied in the Constitution itself.

There is neither doubt nor controversy on the point, that the Fathers of the Republic regarded Slavery as an evil,—as retarding both the material and the moral progress of the Society which tolerated it, as an element of weakness to particular States, and of opprobrium to the whole country. They did not consider slaveholding to be a sin,—nor did they regard a slave-owner as necessarily less moral, less Christian, or less estimable than other men. They did not favor immediate emancipation, because they knew that such a step would be fatal to the negroes themselves, and highly dangerous to the whole fabric of society. But with scarcely an exception,—they all desired that some policy might be adopted looking towards its *ultimate* extinction. These were their sentiments on the general subject. The action of Conventions and of Legislatures, the speeches of statesmen, the correspondence of public men of every grade, and of every section at that early day, abound in evidence of this fact,—which is as clearly and as fully established as any fact of history can possibly be.

With these opinions they came to form a Constitution for the future Republic,—" not for a day but for all time,"—one which should not merely provide for immediate exigencies, but lay the basis of that great Union which it created, and give permament direction to its growth and government. And they embodied in that Constitution just such practical provisions concerning Slavery as their opinions prompted, and as the end aimed at required. The *first* and most conspicuous feature of that policy, was to leave to the several States all jurisdiction over the subject, as being purely one of local authority,—ignoring it entirely as a matter of Federal responsibility. The *second* step was to provide for two exigencies which might arise from its disappearance in some States, and its continued existence in others,—namely the suppression of insurrections, and the return of fugitives. And its *third* was to clothe the General Government with power to prevent the increase of Slavery by prohibiting the importation of slaves after 1808. No person who is entirely disinterested and candid in this matter, can read the Constitution and the history of its formation, without perceiving that this is its general scope and drift. Nor will he doubt for a moment that the universal expectation of that day was, that under this policy Slavery would gradually die out,—that one State after another would take steps to abolish it, and to substitute free labor in its place,—and that thus in the course of time it would cease to exist in the whole country. This purpose was repeatedly declared in Convention and elsewhere ; and no one raised his voice against it. Not even South Carolina nor Georgia, the States which had the largest interest in Slavery, even expressed a wish that it should be made perpetual—and still less did they demand that the Federal Government should guarantee its permanence. Not a voice was raised against the policy of ultimate extinction which was openly avowed, and which the Constitution was so framed as to encourage and favor. The utmost of their claim was that within their own limits it should be left solely and exclusively to their own control. And that claim was conceded to the fullest extent.

This policy thus embodied in the Constitution was accepted by the whole country with alacrity and the active measures of the Government were all framed with a view to carry it into full effect. Through all the successive Administrations of the next quarter of a century the tendency was in the same direction,—and with such occasional exceptions as circumstances rendered unavoidable, its action was towards emancipation. The ordinance of 1787, reënacted by Congress at the very outset of its career, prohibited Slavery from the Northwest Territory. The repeated requests of Indiana to be relieved from this prohibition were refused. In the act organizing the Louisiana Territory, then newly acquired by purchase from France, specific provisions were made forbidding the introduction of slaves except from other States, and then only natives thereof. In 1807 Congress exercised its power, which had been restrained by the Constitution until that time, and under heavy penalties prohibited the importation of slaves from abroad. Not a voice was raised in Congress against the act.

Even the members from Georgia and Carolina concurred in its wisdom and policy,—and the only question that was raised related to the penalties for its violation, and to the manner of disposing of the Africans who might be brought to the country in defiance of law. *Pari passu* with this action of the General Government for the prevention of the increase of Slavery, was that of the State Governments to promote its abolition. Massachusetts, Vermont and Ohio had already prohibited its existence within their limits, and six other States had passed laws providing for gradual and prospective emancipation. Abolition Societies existed in most of the States, and delegates from the South attended regularly at the annual meeting held in Philadelphia. The same general sentiment which had existed at the formation of the Constitution, continued to pervade the whole country. Even Mr. EARLY, the member of Congress from Georgia, whose views on the subject were, perhaps, more ultra than those of any other member, said, in the debate ,on prohibiting the Slave-trade, that, although a large majority of the people in the Southern States did not consider slaveholding as a *crime*, many deprecated it as a political evil,—and that "reflecting men apprehend incalculable evils from it at some future day." And Mr. HOLLAND, of North Carolina, in the same debate, said that " Slavery was *generally* considered a political evil, and that *in that point of view* nearly all were disposed to stop the trade for the future."

This was the sentiment of the whole country, and it continued to animate and guide its action. The Federal Government had gone as far as it had any constitutional power to go in the matter,and the rest was left to the wise discretion of the State Governments, whose control of the subject was conceded to be full and exclusive. And the whole country rested peacefully under this state of things. There was nothing like fanaticism in either section, or among the partisans of either side. Very many men had very strong convictions of hostility to Slavery on moral grounds, but they did not bring those hostilities to the political discussions of the subject. And on the other hand very serious distrust of the free negroes was growing up in those Southern States where the slaves were most numerous, and in some of them it was found necessary to fix such checks on emancipation as should afford some security for the good behavior of those who should be set free. As early as in 1796 North Carolina had forbidden emancipation except for meritorious services. In 1800 South Carolina had required the consent of a justice of the peace and of five disinterested freeholders to the emancipation of any slave ; and even Virginia and Kentucky seriously restrained the liberty of free negroes within their respective limits.

It is not necessary to trace in detail the progress of the change which came over the sentiment of the Southern States on this subject. Owing primarily, without doubt, to the increased culture of

cotton, slave labor became more and more profitable, and the States in which cotton grew became more and more averse to emancipation. Every step away from that original policy of the country led to a corresponding anxiety on the subject in the North. Still the general tendency was towards emancipation. By slower and slower steps, and against increased hostilities, but steadily, nevertheless,—the movement made its way Southward. As late as in 1832 the State of Virginia discussed the subject, and her ablest men boldly and fearlessly pressed upon the people the evils,—material, moral and social, which were inseparable from the institution, and urged the absolute necessity of its removal. Our present Minister in France, Mr. FAULKNER, used language in that Convention in denunciation of Slavery, for which you will find no parallel now, except in the heated harangues of the Abolitionists of the present day. "The idea of a *gradual emancipation* and removal of the slaves from this Commonwealth," said he, " is coeval with the declaration of your own independence from the British yoke."

THE NEW THEORY OF SLAVE PROPERTY IN THE CONSTITUTION.

Down to this period whatever differences existed on the subject of Slavery, there was but one opinion as to its relations under the Constitution to the Federal Government. Mr. CALHOUN introduced a new theory on the subject. He brought forward the doctrine that the Constitution recognized slaves as property,—that, indeed, slaves were the *only* property which was expressly recognized and guaranteed by the Constitution,— and that the slaveholder must therefore be protected in its enjoyment by the power of the Federal Government, wherever he might go within its jurisdiction and under its authority. Upon this principle he must not only have liberty to take his slaves into any Territory of the United States, but must be enabled to hold them there as slaves, by virtue of the Constitution, in spite of any law of Congress or of the Territories which should attempt to forbid it. And that is the principle for which you are contending to-day. At the outset it had very few supporters. No political party, either at the North or South, took ground in its favor. The Democratic Party everywhere scouted it. The people in every section of the country repudiated it with indignation. In spite of the progress it had made in the minds of Southern politicians,—even so lately as last Spring, the Democratic Party of the Union suffered itself to be severed,—dispersed in Convention, and defeated at the polls, rather than give it their assent.

Here is the "irrepressible conflict." It is between the Constitution as our Fathers made it, and the *new* Constitution which you are seeking to put in its place. You are not content with that instrument as it stands, unless you can engraft upon it the new principle,—utterly unknown to its framers, or rather distinctly and intentionally excluded from it by them,—that, namely, of absolute and indefeasible *property* in slaves.

Hitherto you have been contending that this principle is actually embodied in the present Constitution. We ask you where? Point to the section which contains it. You say it is in that section which provides for their representation in Congress. But does the fact that they are *represented* make them property,—or imply that they are property? On the contrary, it implies that *they are not:*—for property is not represented anywhere in our Government. It is one of our boasts that this is a Government of *persons*, and not of *property*,—that it is in the hands of the people,—that the representatives who make its laws and wield its power, are the agents and representatives of persons, and not of property. If this clause, then, constitutes an exception to this general rule, you must show it by something in its language, or by something in the circumstances of the case which leaves no room for doubt. But the language of the clause is directly in the teeth of your claim. The representation specified is that of " three-fifths of all other *persons*,"—besides those mentioned in the previous portion of the sentence. The fact that they are described as persons is at least presumptive evidence that they are not regarded by the Constitution as property; and there is nothing in the circumstances of the case to overthrow that presumption. You may say your local law regards them as property,—and the Federal Constitution must, therefore, regard them in the same light. Not at all;—your local law cannot control the intent of the Constitution, for if it could, all you would have to do in order to change the Constitution would be to change your local law. You may say that though entering into the representation of the country they have no vote,—no voice, no will in its Government,—and that this fact affords a fair implication that they are represented as property. Not at all; for on such a basis your women and children,—who have no vote and are nevertheless represented,—would be property also. But they are taxed, you say, and therefore they are property. No;—they are not taxed, but are only made a means of determining the *ratio* of taxation. Taxation by the Constitution, although paid by property, falls upon property not according to its amount, but according to population;—and when three-fifths of the slaves are counted, therefore, as a basis of taxation, it is only to determine the taxable population and not at all to fix the amount of taxable property.

I can find nothing whatever in this clause, therefore, which gives any show of justice to your claim.

You refer me next to that clause which permits the importation of slaves until 1808,—as proving that they were regarded as subjects of commerce, and therefore as property. The language used does not sustain the assumption. The permission granted is for " the migration or importation of such *persons* as any of the States now existing may think proper to admit." Now this applies just as strongly to the migration or importation of Germans or of Irishmen as of negroes. There is nothing in the language used by which you could determine which was meant. Yet you would scarcely pretend that Germans or Irishmen "imported" under that permission became thereby *property*; yet the presumption in the one case would be just as strong as in the other.

Finally, you cite the Fugitive Slave clause as conclusive proof that slaves are property in the intendment of the Constitution. That clause simply declares that " persons held to service or labor in one State, under the laws thereof, escaping into another," shall be delivered up. They are *cal'ed* persons; in what word or phrase do you find the implication that they are regarded as property? Does the fact that they are " held to service or labor " make them property? Certainly not,—for apprentices, minors, and day-laborers are held to service or labor,—and yet they do not thereby become property. Does the fact that they are to be " delivered up " make them property? Certainly not,—for fugitives from justice are also, by a preceding clause, to be delivered up,—and yet nobody pretends that this fact makes *them* property.

Now these are all the clauses of the Constitution in which slaves are referred to in any way,—and there is nothing in any one of them which gives the least countenance to your claim. They are represented as persons and not as property; they were imported as persons, and not as property; they are to be delivered up, when they escape, as persons, and not as property.

THE REAL ISSUE AND THE NECESSITY OF DECIDING IT.

The real question at issue between the North and South, (using these terms as convenient designations of the two opposing parties,) turns upon this point—which involves all others—*are slaves property*, in the meaning and intendment of the Constitution? *Do they stand in the view, and under the provisions, of that instrument, on the same footing as other property?* You answer Yes; we answer No. And you are threatening to dissolve the Union unless we will also answer Yes. Nay, more,—you are already endeavoring to dissolve it, because we persist in answering No!

This is the question which I think should be finally settled now. I think the whole country is of the same opinion. Undoubtedly there are a great many persons in both sections who deprecate joining issue upon it. They prefer that it should be evaded or compromised. Some of them dread the disturbance—the damage to business—the alienation of feelings—the possible perils and devastations of war to which a final settlement of the question may give rise. Others underrate its importance, and see no reason why the great current of our national prosperity should be interrupted, in order to settle an abstract point of constitutional interpretation. But I think the great body of the reflecting portion of the people regard it in a different light. They know that the issue is one of principle,—that it takes hold on the fundamental conditions of the national life,—and that until it is distinctly and decisively settled, by a final and authoritative judgment, in which the whole country shall come to acquiesce, we can have no hope of peace and no chance of escape from these constant and disturbing agitations. If the difference were trifling in its nature, or temporary in its effect, there would be no such necessity. It might then be compromised. But it is vital. Its decision stamps the character of our Government, and gives a direction to its policy which it must keep to the end of its existence. If your demands be complied with, Slavery becomes one of the essential, ineradicable elements of our national life—just as vital and as permanent in it as the principle of Republicanism, as freedom of speech, trial by jury, or freedom of religious worship. Your aim is, in the sharp, clear phrase of the day, to *nationalize Slavery*—to make it a national instead of a local institution—not necessarily for the purpose of carrying *slaves* into every part of the country, but to make the supreme law of every part *slave law*. You demand that Slavery shall no longer stand as an exceptional institution, ignored by the General Government, frowned upon by civilization, and under the ban of Christendom—but that it shall take its fixed place as only one form of the eternal institution of Property ; that, as the law of Real Estate, and the law of Chattel Property, are recognized as fixed and enduring parts of the great code of the world, so the Law of Slave Property shall have its place, equally stable and equally honorable, wherever the flag of the United States, and the power which that flag symbolizes and represents, can compel its recognition.

Now this is not a point to be compromised. It never has been compromised, nor will it ever be—because it is, in its nature, incapable of compromise. Our country must be one thing or the other. Our Constitution must either thus recognize Slavery, or it must not. All our compromises hitherto, numerous and important as they have been, have evaded this great central point of the whole subject. They have all turned on questions of temporary and local expediency ;—whether Slavery should exist in this place or in that ;—by what forms and by whose agency fugitive slaves should be recaptured ; into which sectional scale the political weight of this or that new State should be thrown ; whether we should make this or that addition to our national Territory, even at the risk of increasing the area of Slavery. All these issues have arisen and have been settled on the basis of compromise. But none of them involved the great point at which nevertheless all of them aimed. They were the approaches to the citadel,—tentative demonstrations towards conquering the Constitution ;—but every one of them might have been yielded without actually giving

up that still unconquered Malakoff of Liberty. But now you have brought your batteries to the central tower, and we are summoned to surrender. That question does not admit of compromise. It must be settled. The flag of Liberty must still float from the ramparts of the Constitution, or you must take it down. This is the "irrepressible conflict." We do not make it,—nor invite it ;—but if you insist upon it, we shall not shrink from its issues.

WHAT IS SLAVERY IN THE CONSTITUTION ?

But this, you say, is making war upon Slavery ; —this discards and ignores all the Constitutional guarantees of Slavery :—this is an open declaration of hostility to the institutions of the Southern States. Not at all. You are putting an interpretation upon it growing out of your own theories based upon your own assumptions,—not warranted by the fact. We are perfectly willing to take the Constitution as it stands,—to leave Slavery upon the basis which it provides for it, and to fulfil every obligation, express or implied, which it imposes. And in determining what those obligations are, we look first for a *Constitutional definition of Slavery*,—as the treatment of the subject must depend upon its nature : and we find the definition, in just such clear and precise terms the Constitution always employs, in the following clause :

"No *person held to service or labor in one State, under the laws thereof*, escaping into another, shall, in consequence of any law or regulation therein, be discharged from such service or labor, but shall be delivered up on claim of the party to whom such service or labor may be due."

We regard this as the definition which the Constitution gives to the word slave,—or, which amounts to the same thing, as the phrase which the framers of the Constitution employed as, in their judgment, synonymous with that word. And it establishes these points :

1. A slave is a PERSON.

2. The characteristic feature of his condition that which distinguishes him from other persons, is that he is "held to service or labor," not by contract, but by law.

3. This legal holding to service or labor is in a *State*,—and "under the laws *thereof*;"—that is,—the condition of a slave is created and maintained only by the law of the locality or State in which he is "held,"—not by any law common to all localities, or all States.

4. Under all ordinary circumstances, and in the absence of any provision to the contrary, whenever the slave should leave that State in which, and "under the law" of which he is "held,"—he might be discharged from his "service" in, and by the law of, the new locality into which he should enter. The Constitution provides, therefore, that he shall not be thus discharged on two conditions,—(1) that this new locality be another State, and (2) that he has "escaped" into it.

There is the "Slave-code" of the Constitution.

That is the basis on which Slavery rests, so far as the Constitution of the United States is concerned. If Slavery anywhere implies anything more than this, it must be by virtue of some local law. If Slavery in Georgia or South Carolina is something more than this, it must be by force of some law of Georgia or South Carolina. This is all that the Federal Constitution knows about a slave—the full extent to which it goes in recognizing his slave-condition. The language is perfectly clear and unmistakable, so far as its definition of Slavery, in its relations to the Federal Government, is concerned. In its positive provisions for " delivering up " the fugitive slave, it becomes ambiguous. It leaves in doubt the points by what authority, and under ˙)at forms, the fugitive is to be " delivered up,' ,ether by Federal authority or by State authority ⁴ under the provisions of the common law. ı̇on these points there is room for doubt, and ˛sibly a necessity for greater explicitness ; but ˙ıt explicitness, if it be afforded, must conform to ˛p previous definition—not violate or overthrow

THE IRREPRESSIBLE CONFLICT.

ı̇You are in the habit of charging the North with ˛ıving produced all the sectional discontent that ˛ºw prevails by departing from the Constitution. ˛will not say that there is no truth in the allega-_ion. Possibly we have, in some particulars, been ıss rigid in adhering to that instrument than we ˙ıould have been. But none of these deviations ˛ı our part will compare with that great change ˙ıhich you demand in its essential elements and ˛haracter. Nor have they caused your discontent. ˛.s I have already shown in these letters, it is ˙ıot our Personal Liberty bills, nor our failure to ˛urrender fugitives, nor the practical inability of ˛ıaveholders to take their slaves into the Territories, that creates the difficulty. *That difficulty has ˛rown out of your determination to make a new* ˛*Constitution.* It is due primarily, and therefore ˛ntirely, to your departure from the policy of the ˛Fathers of the Republic, as that policy was embodied in the Constitution,—as it stands revealed in the ˛language of that instrument, and interpreted by the opinions and sentiments of the men who made it. You demand that principles shall be engrafted upon it which they carefully and intentionally excluded from it. As you stated in your Montgomery speech " *an entirely new idea has sprung up in the South*" on the subject of Slavery,—and you demand that this new idea shall be embodied in the Constitution. Hitherto, to be sure, you have sought this end by construction,—by legislation,—by the language of party platforms,—by decrees of the Supreme Court, rather than by open and direct amendments. But now you insist upon the reconstruction of the Constitution itself, and the adoption into its language of the ideas and principles for which you contend. The " irrepressible conflict" is, therefore, not between the North and the South,—but between the South and the Constitution. You have found the present Constitution, so far as your purposes are concerned, a failure. Unless, therefore, it can be overthrown by am**E**ndments, you are determined to overthrow it *by force.* I do not think you will succeed in either.

THE DUTY OF THE NORTH.

Now, what is to be done ? You have brought the issue to its present point. As a matter of necessity and of policy, you seek to throw the whole blame of the controversy upon the North. If we had not resisted your claims, there would have been no sectional contest. That is perfectly true ; and it is also true, that if you had not made these claims, we should not have resisted them. But since you *have* made them, and since we do resist them, the conflict must go on until one party or the other recedes, or is defeated. I see no possible way of avoiding this. But a great deal may be done towards creating a conciliatory disposition on both sides—towards inducing each party to lay aside something of its passion, something of its obstinate adhesion to its own views on minor matters, and to canvass the grounds of the controversy in the light of principle, of the Constitution, of the highest good of the whole country and of all its parts,—instead of the prejudices, the arrogance and the pride of any section. So far as my experience. and reading go, they teach me that very few controversies between communities or individuals have ever arisen, that did not rest *au fond* on a misunderstanding,—and that did not grow into formidable proportions more from the introduction into them of minor exasperations from alien causes, than from any inherent impossibility of agreeing on the precise point involved. I think it is so to some extent in the present case ; and that the first duty of each section is first to adjust or sweep away all minor points of difference,—to calm the fever of passion, to open wide the door to a mutual knowledge of each other's real sentiments, wants and purposes, and to bring to the council board a real wish to find the path of honor and of safety for both. What, then, is the duty of the North in this respect ?

Its first duty, in my judgment, is to manifest its desire to accommodate the rational and conservative men of the South by whatever concessions and compromises their actual necessities may require, and which can be given without surrendering the vital principle which is involved. In regard to the Fugitive Slave law, for example, the North should unquestionably fulfill the obligation which the Constitution imposes,—in its letter, where that is possible, and in its spirit, where nothing more can be accomplished. Every fugitive from service should be delivered up ; and where, from violence, or any other cause for which the North or any portion of its people are clearly responsible, this endeavor is defeated, they should compensate the person to whom the service or labor of the fugitive was due, for the pecuniary loss he may have sustained in consequence of **that** default. You may say this is not a fulfillment of the obligation :—that the Constitution requires the absolute surrender of the fugitive, at all hazards,—and that any scheme of compensation is only an evasion. But you would not apply this unbending rule to any other subject. All laws are to be obeyed literally,—but in case of their violation or default, the law itself, as well as common sense, accepts damages as the equivalent. The object of the Fugitive Slave law is to protect the slaveholder from loss on account of the escape of the person " owing him service or labor" into another State :—and if this object cannot be attained by the literal delivery of the fugitive, compensation is all that remains. A railroad company is bound to transport its passengers in safety : it contracts to do so. But if it breaks a passenger's leg, it responds in damages, and is held acquitted. Even if slaves were property, this would be all you could claim in law or in equity.

So in regard to invasions of the Southern States ; the North is in duty bound to give such practical guarantees as the case admits against them. The duty of the North on this point is very clearly and emphatically set forth in the fourth article of the Platform of the Republican Party adopted at Chicago,—in these terms :

" That the maintenance inviolate of the rights of the States, and especially the right of each State to order and control its own domestic institutions according to its own judgment, EXCLUSIVELY, is essential to that balance of power on which the perfection and endurance of our political fabric depends :—and we denounce the lawless invasion by armed force of any State or Territory, no matter under what pretext, as among the GRAVEST OF CRIMES."

This is the doctrine of the Administration which comes into power on the 4th of March next. It pledges the Republican Party to practical measures for the suppression of such invasions ; and I think it is the duty of that party to bring forward a law in Congress which shall make every such attempt to overthrow the sovereign authority of any state, by armed invasion from any other State, a grave crime against the Federal Government, and to punish it accordingly. As the law now stands, such invasions are offences only against the States invaded. JOHN BROWN and his associates were tried and executed under the laws of Virginia. The crime was primarily against that State,—but it ought also to have been a crime against the Federal Government, which exists in part for the very purpose of promoting the general tranquillity. I would not have Congress go so far as was proposed by Senator DOUGLAS last Winter, to punish any conspiracy in one State to entice away slaves from any other,—for this, besides encountering still more formidable objections, would involve an unwarrantable and dangerous extension of Federal power into the domestic concerns of the individual States. But any armed invasion from one State, for the purpose of overthrowing the laws and contesting the sovereignty of any other, ought to be suppressed and punished by the Federal authority.

So, also, should the North make full provision for the suppression of negro insurrections in any Southern State. The Constitution imposes upon the General Government the duty of suppressing insurrection, and no one doubts that servile insurrections are included in the obligation. Undoubtedly the duty rests in the first instance upon the State of enforcing its own laws,—but where its power should prove inadequate, especially in presence of so formidable and horrible a form of danger as a rebellion of slaves involves, it should receive the aid of the Federal arm. Southern writers are in the habit of speaking of Northern communities as eager to plunge the South into the horrors of servile war,—as indifferent to the nameless deeds of butchery and outrage which such a war would involve, and to the general ruin which it would bring in its train. There could be no more serious error. The great mass of the people of the North look upon such contingencies with the same shuddering horror that moves the South. Their sympathies are with their brethren of the same race, and they would lend their aid promptly and cheerfully, if it should be needed, to defend them from such catastrophes. If there are any misgivings on the part of the South on this subject, which judicious action of the Federal Government could allay, I have no doubt that the North would readily assent. We have no interests to be served,—no resentments to be gratified,—no aims to be promoted by the forcible overthrow of Southern society or the violent rupture of Southern institutions. On the contrary, whatever helps the South helps us. Whatever builds up her prosperity builds up ours. We share her success, her burdens and her shame. And we should never stand by and see her peace assailed, and her existence threatened, by foreign or domestic foes, without coming to her aid.

THE TERRITORIAL QUESTION.

Now here are three points which touch most nearly the interests and the safety of the slaveholding States,—especially of those which lie along the Northern border :—and on each of them I think the North would readily agree to do what all must concede to be substantially just and right.

Another point of difference arises in regard to the Territories—into which men from both North and South may wish to emigrate. They are the property of the United States,—and the people of each State have an undivided, and pro rata an equal, interest in their ownership. It is clearly right that every citizen who goes into them should stand there upon an equal legal footing with every other citizen :—that whatever one may lawfully take into them another may,—and that if one is prohibited from taking any special thing, every other citizen should be prohibited from taking the same thing also. So long as this rule is observed, it would not seem possible that any complaint of inequality could be made,—for inequality of rights implies that some things are conceded as rights to one class of persons and denied to another class. Nothing of this sort obtains in this case. A Southern man can take into the Territories whatever a Northern man can, and when there, both stand on an equal footing.

There is no difficulty in recognizing this perfect equality of rights that obtains between the two, so long as the question is thus limited to specific *things :*—it is only when some general term is used which includes many *different* things, that doubts and differences arise. Every one can see that the Southern man may take into the Territories a horse, a half-eagle, a carriage or a cart,—and that a Northern man may take precisely the same things,—both thus standing upon precisely the same footing. But when you ask if each may take his *property* with him, you employ a term that needs defining:—and when you analyze it you find that it embodies two separate and distinct ideas,—first, the thing itself,—and second, the legal relations of that thing. Thus, if two men go to Kansas, each accompanied by a negro,—the first question that arises on their arrival is, what is the relation of each to the negro who is with him ? One of the two asserts that his negro is his *property,*—because the law of Alabama from which he came made him so. The claim therefore, is that he brings with him not only the negro,—but also the *local law* of the State from which he comes, and on which he relies to establish their relations. The man from Vermont can claim no such right, because he has no such local law to bring. The inequality of their condition, therefore, grows entirely out of the inequality in the laws of the States from which they come ;—and the real question is, *whether that inequality shall be transferred to the Territories,* or whether both shall leave behind them their discordant State laws, and submit to the uniform and equal laws which the Sovereign Authority, whatever it may be, may enact for the government of the Territories.

You say your local law has vested in you an absolute right of property in your slaves,—and that you have the right, therefore, to take the creations of that law with you. But you would not apply the principle to any other form of property. A State law may give you a vested property right in a bank charter, a lottery, a railroad or a steamboat charter, —but that right would be valid only within the geographical jurisdiction of that law. No law can give rights beyond the boundaries of its own authority. You say the Constitution of the United States recognizes that vested right, and thus gives it universality. Upon that point we join issue. We deny that there is any such recognition,—and the grounds of that denial I have already stated in the preceding part of this letter. But you say this is depriving us of our *property,*—or of the right to take our property with us into the Territories. Not at all. It only deprives you of the right to take your property in a particular, exceptional *form*—given to it solely by your local law. You can convert it, while under the operation and protection of that local law, into another, a larger, uni-

versal form, and thus take it with you wherever you wish to go. You can sell your slaves and take with you the money, which as property is their equivalent.

The whole difference in regard to the Territories thus turns on the point whether the absolute *right of property* in slaves is, or is not, recognized in the Constitution. Indeed this is the entire scope, —the real heart and marrow, of the whole controversy between the North and South. And upon this point I see no possibility of compromise. I do not believe that, under any circumstances, the North will ever concede the *right* to take slaves *as property under the Constitution* into the Territories. I do not believe they will ever consent to engraft upon the Constitution a recognition of slave property which the framers of that instrument carefully excluded from it. On this point I think the great mass of the people of the Northern States are immovable,—and in my judgment they could not be otherwise without running upon evils of the most perilous magnitude. You are in the habit of insisting upon this recognition as a matter of small importance,—as intended merely to give you an equal right to the enjoyment of the Territorial property of the common Union, and as so palpably just, that it can only be denied from a motive of contempt for the Constitution and for your rights under it. But you know that this is not so. You know very well that, if the Constitution be so amended as to recognize this absolute, indefeasible right of property in slaves,—these consequences will follow :

1. Any man may take a Slave into any *Territory,* and hold him and his posterity there as Slaves forever,—and the Federal Government must protect him in so doing.

2. Any man may take a Slave into any *State,* and hold him and his posterity as Slaves there forever, under the protection of the Federal Government ; for the Constitution provides in express terms that no citizen shall be deprived of his property except by due process of law,—and this provision like all others in the Constitution is to be the supreme law of the land, anything in the Constitution or laws of any State to the contrary notwithstanding.

3. No slaveholding State will have any right to provide by law for the emancipation of its slaves, without the consent of every owner, for that would be a direct, unconstitutional interference with the right of property.

4. Slaves being thus made property by the Constitution, must become the subjects of commerce, domestic and foreign, on the same footing as other property, and subject only to the same regulations and restrictions as may be applied to all property alike. The laws of Congress, prohibiting the importation of slaves,—being inconsistent with this Constitutional provision, become inoperative and void.

To indicate these results of the principle you wish us to recognize is sufficient, without further argument, to show why it can never be admitted by the Constitution, either by express amendment or by legislation that will imply its existence. And this is one of the reasons, perhaps the controlling one, why the people of the North will never consent to the extension of Slavery into the Territories as a matter of right.

I do not mean to say that they might not, under the pressure of circumstances, and in presence of some great necessity, assent to some compromise on this subject, which would leave some portion of the Federal territory open to Slavery. But any such assent must rest wholly on grounds of expediency, and not upon the claim of Constitutional right.

It is a general impression at the South that the motive of the North in resisting the extension of Slavery is a desire to " pen it up,"—to confine it within a small area, and let it there " sting itself to death,"—in other words, become so dangerous to society as to compel its abolition as a measure of self-defence. Undoubtedly this is a motive with many men,—but I do not believe it to be a controlling motive with the North. I do not believe there are five States in the Union a majority of whose people would vote for an immediate, unprepared emancipation of the Southern Slaves, if that emancipation depended exclusively on their votes. And still less would they vote to compel that emancipation by measures which must involve Southern white society in disaster and ruin. Our people do not seek to restrict Slavery in order to suffocate it. Their hostility to its practical extension rests on a regard for the welfare of the Territories,—an unwillingness to increase the political power of Slavery,—and a determination to do nothing which shall make it perpetual and paramount in our Federal Councils. But if the time should ever come when the South, for its own safety, needs an outlet for its surplus slave population, I do not believe the North would oppose such migration into some Territorial region adapted to it. Indeed, most men at the North who reflect upon the subject at all, look to the gradual drifting of Slavery Southward,—both within and without the present limits of the Union, as the only way in which it can ever be removed.

But whenever this is done, it must be done solely as a measure of expediency, and not as a matter of Constitutional right. Nor, in my judgment, will the People ever consent that the Federal Government shall protect slave property in any Territories regardless of the will of their inhabitants,— or that any amendments shall be made to the Constitution changing the basis of Slavery, or substituting any new definition of the *status* of a slave. In other words, I do not believe that threats of Disunion, attempts at Disunion, or even the complete accomplishment of Disunion, would induce the North to give Slavery any clearer recognition, or any higher place, in the Federal Constitution, than it has at present. We ask you to abide by that Constitution.' We demand nothing more.

Take it as our Fathers made it. They yielded much for the sake of the Union,—but you have no reason to believe that they would have yielded more, even from that high motive. No man then dared or desired to propose that property in slaves should be recognized and stand on the same footing, in all federal and constitutional relations, as any other species of property ;—and if he had made the demand you cannot believe it would have been conceded. The Union is less essential now to our national greatness and prosperity than it was then. The people are stronger and have more confidence in their strength, and they will not concede now what would never have been conceded then.

THE NORTHERN DENUNCIATIONS OF SLAVERY—HOW THEY CAN BE SILENCED AND SUPPRESSED.

But there still remains one grievance against which you demand security,—the *denunciations of Slavery in the Northern States.* You complain that they are dangerous and offensive,—that they violate the comity which should obtain between members of the same Union, and that they wound the pride and the self-respect of the South. And you insist that they shall be stopped. The Press, the Pulpit, the high places of political power, members of Congress and State Legislatures, Governors, lecturers, school books, poetry, history, novels,—all forms of literature and of speech are regarded as offenders in this respect. All breathe a tone of hostility to Slavery incompatible with its peaceful existence, and destructive of all friendly relations between the States.

The complaint finds some warrant in the facts of the case. But if you seek a practical remedy you, must look to the origin and the nature of the disease. Some few of your publicists are insane enough to suppose that it can be cured by legislative coercion. The result of the experiment which you made in 1835 upon the Right of Petition,— one of the smallest features of the general tendency, and one moreover which Congress had under its complete control, must show the folly of such a hope,—even if all history and all philosophy were not eloquent against it. You would find it infinitely easier to reduce every Northern State to the condition of an abject provincial dependency of South Carolina, than to expel this habit of free speech from the Northern mind. Menaces of displeasure, threats of Disunion, acts of retaliation, simply heap fuel on the raging flames. You may exhort, remonstrate and reason with us on the subject. You may appeal to our sense of justice and of fair-dealing, and we will listen to the plea,—either acquiescing in its equity or exposing its weakness. You have it in your power to make the appeal availing,—and it lies in the direction of *removing the causes and provocations* of the hostile censures of which you complain. I do not mean by this that you must abolish Slavery, though unquestionably while Slavery exists it will be denounced. But if you would silence these hot and blistering censures of the world, you must reform the system, and relieve it of many of its present features.

You do not seem to be at all aware of the character and tendencies of the Civil Society you are building up in the Southern States. It is not the mere *fact* of Slavery that constitutes its distinguishing feature,—but the *kind* of Slavery, and the influence it is exerting over the legislation, the morals and manners, the thoughts and opinions of Southern Society. When you read a few years ago Mr. GLADSTONE'S revelations of the nature of the Government of Naples,—how all freedom of speech was suppressed, how men were imprisoned or exiled for uttering thoughts of liberty, or censures of official acts,—how all free participation in public affairs was denied, and political activity rigidly restricted to the tools of the tyranny that ruled,— how the forms of justice were abused to the purposes of oppression, and all society was subjected to the authority of force, aiming only at the absolute and perpetual supremacy of a single, selfish interest, you had no difficulty in predicting the ruin of such a system and the utter overthrow of the power on which it rested. You judge of the security of all foreign governments by the degree to which they enlist the favor and friendly support of their subjects. When the welfare of the masses is consulted and their rights respected,—wherever the supreme authority makes the people its allies and aids, the Government is safe, because it has disarmed those who are liable to become its enemies. But when the heavy hand of power is the only weapon used,—when justice means simply the welfare and the will of the dominant authority, you know perfectly well the fate which must overtake it. You can read the coming doom of Austria in Venetia in the character of the sway she has established there. You can see how idle it is to ask that the people of Piedmont, enjoying freedom themselves, should not denounce and execrate the despotism that crushes life and hope from the hearts of their immediate neighbors. What fatal delusion blinds you to the same sad lesson, when it glares at you from the pages of your own legislation ?

TENDENCIES OF SOUTHERN CIVIL SOCIETY.

The worst tyranny of the worst Government which ever existed is fairly paralleled in the current history of the Southern States. No man within your borders dare canvass fairly and publicly the wisdom of the leading feature of your own Society. In this Republican Government, where the people choose their rulers, no man dare to-day avow openly in the Southern States that he voted for the man who has been elected President of the Republic. Freedom of speech, freedom of opinion, freedom of political action, are more thoroughly stifled and extinguished in the South than in Austria, or Russia, or the most absolute despotism on the face of the earth. And a still worse feature of the case is, that this

violence does not even think it necessary to clothe itself in the forms of law. It is not by legal tribunals,—not by ministers of justice, nor even under pretence of legality, that these awful outrages on the spirit of liberty are perpetrated. In all other lands despotism puts on the robes of legal form. It clothes itself in the outward garb of law, even when it perpetrates the worst outrages upon its spirit. But in the South it repudiates all restraint,—all form,—all respect for the opinions of the world. It stalks abroad like a hideous savage,—scornful of civilization, obeying only the impulse of its brutal nature, and lording it over courts and magistrates as imperiously as over the meaner subjects of its rule. You say these lawless outrages are perpetrated only by the mob, the scum and ruffianism of the community. But where are the orderly,—the respectable, the civilized and law-abiding portion of your people ? Either they approve of these acts, or they submit to them from stern necessity, and because they dare not oppose them. In either case the result is the same. They are silent and powerless. They have no voice in the Government of their own society. And unless all history is false, nothing is more certain, than that they will become victims of that savage Despotism which they are powerless to withstand,—against which they dare not even protest. Every year their danger becomes more imminent, because the causes which create it become more potent. They have surrendered the authority which they ought to wield with prudence, with wisdom, and with due regard to the tendencies and influences of the age, into the hands of brutal, reckless force,—which ignores all equity, scoffs at all moral influences and tramples like a beast upon everything that stands in the way of its will.

One immediate practical result of this policy is, that the great mass of your people perform their most important political duties, in utter ignorance of the facts most essential to their just and intelligent discharge. Take the recent Presidential canvass as an example. Mr. LINCOLN was a candidate for the Presidency. You asserted throughout the South, that he was in favor of the abolition of slavery ;—that he regarded the negro as the equal of the white man, and was in favor of giving him equal social and political rights ;—that he and the party which supported him were pledged to open and deadly hostility against the South,—and that his success would be the signal of your ruin. The truth of these assertions was the most important point involved in the contest,—especially to the people of the Southern States. Did you allow it' to be freely and fairly canvassed? Your local journals echoed the assertion and closed their columns to anything that would discredit it. Your postmasters,—or rather the Federal postmasters upon your soil,—refused to deliver journals that denied and refuted it. You ignored or confiscated and destroyed the public speeches of Mr. LINCOLN himself, by which its truth or falsehood could have been decisively tested. You admitted from abroad no newspapers but those which echoed and re-affirmed the abominable slander, and you lynched every man at home who ventured to dispute it. The effect of all this may be illustrated by a single incident.

I received a private letter not many days ago from an intelligent, upright, fair-minded and influential gentleman,—holding high public station in the State of Mississippi,—in which he closed some remarks on the election by saying: —" And when I say that I would regard death by a stroke of lightning to Mr. Lincoln as just punishment from an offended Deity for his infamous and unpatriotic avowals, *especially those made on a presentation of a pitcher by some free negroes to Gov. Chase, of Ohio*, you may judge how less just and temperate men feel." Now I have it on authority which you would not question, that "Mr. Lincoln never *saw Gov. Chase in his life ;—*that *he never attended a meeting of negroes, free or slave, in his life ;—and that he never saw a pitcher presented by anybody to anybody*." But the statement was published, originally, so far as I know, in the New-York *Herald*,—and circulated throughout the South. No denial or correction was allowed to follow it. What people or what nation can exercise the right of self-government with judgment or justice, when they are thus shut up without defence to the power of systematic falsehood? You fastened upon us the epithet of *Black Republicans ;—*you have circulated the falsehood that our candidate for Vice President has negro blood in his veins ;—you might have asserted with the same impunity, that we were all negroes,—for you would have found Northern journalists and politicians base enough to countenance the lie, and your domestic regulations would have prevented its effectual contradiction among the masses of the people in the Southern States. Do you believe that such a political system is consistent with safety ?

CHARACTER AND TENDENCY OF THE SYSTEM OF SLAVERY.

I have referred thus far solely to the tyranny exercised over the white portion of Southern society as one of the causes which provoke the denunciations of which you complain. I know very well, however, that it grows out of, and is inseparable from, the system of government you have adopted for your slaves. I have no wish to enter upon the details of that system. My object is merely to designate its leading features, and I make no enumeration, therefore, of the countless illustrations of the system afforded in the every-day life of the Southern plantation. The whole system rests on the assumption that the negro is not a man,—that he is, if not absolutely a brute, at best a link between the human and the brute creation ;—and that his place in society is that of absolute subjection to the will not only of a master, but of an owner ;—and that all the arrangements of society must be such as will keep him and his descendants

forever in that position. This assumption repudiates everything like *rights* in connection with the negro. He has no right to his wife or to his children any more than to himself. He has no right to any degree of freedom, either in action, i speech or in hope. He has no right to instructio —to moral culture,—to the development of wha ever faculties he may possess, or even to physic support and comfort. Whatever he may enjoy of au of these things, is the voluntary gift of his owner, prompted either by his own interest, by his huma ity, or his personal sense of obligation, not co ceded at all as a matter of right on the part of the slave. And the tendency of this system in its practical workings is steadily towards greater and greater rigor. The arm of power becomes muscular and heavy by being used. The regulations for slaves become more and more severe, as their severity provokes open or sullen discontent. The privileges accorded to them become less and less. State laws are becoming more and more common prohibiting their emancipation. Masters who are indulgent become more and more objects of suspicion and hostility. They are felt to be out of place in the system,—incongruous with its spirit and dangerous to its permanent existence. The grand point to be established in its theory and in its practical working is, that *the will of a white man*,—without any regard to the thing willed,—without regard to its justice, its right or wrong, its humanity or barbarity, its necessity or its uselessness,—the *bare will* of the white is to be, in all cases and under all contingencies, *the absolute, supreme law for the negro*, against which it is treason to rebel, and resistance to which may be punished with whatever tortures the authority that makes the law may see fit to inflict. This is the essence of the American slave system as it exists in theory, and in law, in the Southern States. I do not say that there are no departures from that theory in practice. There are departures from it,—not only in isolated cases, but in whole communities, and in many entire States. But there are also States in which the practical workings of the system have already come closely up to its theory. And the *tendency* is steadily in that direction. The despotism over the whites, of which I have already spoken, is designed to crush out all these exceptional cases, and to make American Slavery in practice and in fact what it is in the theory on which it rests.

You must not understand me as implying that the Federal Government, or that we of the North, have any right to interpose our power against this tendency in the slaveholding States. You are sov ereign over your own domestic affairs, of which this is one. But you are demanding the sanction of the Federal Government for it all. You are seeking to graft upon the Constitution the principle which lies at the bottom of it all,—out of which it all grows just as naturally as a forest of oaks grows out of a single acorn,—namely, that *a slave is property and nothing e'se*. And you are demanding also that we of the North shall cease denouncing or censuring a system under which these things are possible,—nay, under which, according to your own excuse for them, they are necessary and inevitable. For this is your plea in their defence. Without them, you assert, Slavery is impossible,—because no system less rigid, less exacting, less despotic, could keep the slaves in subjection.

THE CERTAINTY THAT SUCH A SYSTEM MUST FAIL.

Now if this plea is true, it affords the most conclusive demonstration that the system is doomed to speedy destruction—and the only question that remains is, whether that destruction shall come amid the nameless enormities of a wholesale slaughter, or in some less formidable shape. If you will separate yourself from all connection with it, and look upon it as you would upon any other social problem or phenomenon in which you had no personal concern or preconceived opinion, I think you would have little difficulty in seeing, and little hesitation in saying, that such a system in North America, and in this advanced age of civilization, could not possibly be made permanent. Upon some remote island in some distant sea—far removed from all contact with the sentiments, the movements, the active moral and material agencies of the world, a weak tribe of ignorant savages might be thus permanently held under the supreme will of a dominant race. But under no other conditions is it possible. The same powers, visible and invisible, which have changed the face of other communities, must have sway in the South. The railroad, the telegraph, the steamboat, printing, public discussion, inventions—these are among the agencies which have given so great an impulse to the principle of liberty all over the world within the last half century. The general effect of them all is to rouse the mind to action—to stimulate the moral energies and the self-asserting elements of character, in every community which they pervade. No man can live for years in full sight of a Railroad, and witness daily the power which its operations indicate, without being changed in some of the most essential elements of his character. It shames his weakness,—it widens the circle of his thoughts,—it gives dignity and a larger scope to his aspirations and his aims. So is it with all the great agencies of civilization. Now you have all of these things in the Southern States, and you must continue to have them. They all symbolize power, freedom, the unchecked development of human energy, and they all point to loftier hopes and endeavors. Do you suppose that your slaves can be shut out from these influences, or that they can be exposed to them and remain the same tame beasts of burden which they were at the outset? Take especially that great agency of Popular Education, the political discussions of the day. Do you suppose your negroes go through such a campaign as the one just closed with no new ideas —no fresh impulses—no other hopes and longings

c

than they had before? Can they hear you discuss the great themes of liberty and labor—the stirring questions of peace and war—the issues of Tariffs and Homestead bills and Railroads, the importance of cotton and sugar and rice to the movements of the world, the relations of the races, the possibilities and prospects of emancipation, the views and sentiments of the different political parties upon all these topics, and yet be in thought, in feeling and in character precisely what they were before the campaign commenced? Do you observe no difference in the spirit, the intelligence and the temper of those slaves who live in large towns and have been brought in constant contact with all these influences, and those who live on the remote plantations of the back country, seeing and hearing of nothing but their daily task? And has it not occurred to you that the causes of this difference are operating steadily and irresistibly upon the great masses of the people, Slaves included, everywhere,—and that sooner or later they will transform them into something very different from what they find them?

In the policy of Repression and Force, which is the policy to which the South seems inclined to commit its destiny, she is making precisely the mistake which has ruined every Despotism on the face of the earth,—against which History and Philosophy alike protest,—and which can have but one result,—the ruin and destruction of all concerned. You can see this in foreign societies: why are you so utterly blind to it in your own? One after another the dominations that rest on Power alone break through the thin and fragile crust, and disappear forever. To the careless eye their foundation seems solid and seamless as the ice that congeals and covers the lake. But steadily and silently decay works upon the under surface, and the gale of a night sweeps away the last vestige of what seemed adamant the day before. What is to make the South an exception to this universal law? Is it that the slaves are black? So were those of St. Domingo. Is it that black blood and brain have no capacity to plan revolt? Even if this plea were true, the white blood mingling with the black blood of the South is rapidly giving them leaders for every emergency. It gives eyes and thought to the blind Polyphemus that seems to be lying helpless and prone. Is it that your power is too compact,—your supremacy too thoroughly established,—your measures of repression too vigorous and comprehensive to permit such a catastrophe? Alas! so thought the King of Naples,—so thinks every despot down to the very hour that precipitates his doom.

No power on earth is adequate to the permanent suppression of the moral forces that sway the world. You may divert the force but you cannot suppress it. And the course upon which the South has entered, if steadily pursued, is just as certain to end in ruin, as fastening down the safety-valve of a steam boiler is to end in an explosion.

It may not come in five, or in ten, or in fifty years :—but it is just as inevitable as Fate. You may not live to be its victim, but your children will.

I am not in this predicting what I wish should happen. Far from it. I am only stating the necessary result of an irresistible law. Nor am I claiming any authority on the part of the Federal Government to interfere with it. The Constitution has given control of it exclusively to your own States. All that the Federal Government can do is to look on—sadly and with a clear foresight of the certain issue—and when the catastrophe comes—interfere on your behalf and for your protection. But you cannot expect or ask us to look on in silence. You cannot expect us to utter no warning, to put forth no remonstrance, to feel and express no indignation at a blindness so obstinate and so fatal. If you would silence the Pulpit and the Press of the North, you must disarm them. You must remove the causes which justly provoke their denunciations. I know no other way of attaining the object you seek. Possibly they ought to desist without these conditions. I doubt not you think they should, and deem it discourteous and hostile that they will not. But the fact remains. Just so long as you continue to affront the instinctive sense of justice and humanity by a policy which imitates and transcends the worst illustrations of despotism the world has ever seen, just so long will you rouse the resentment, and incur the censure, not only of the North, but of every nation of Christendom. If it be your object, therefore, to secure immunity from these didactic hostilities,—if you wish practically to escape, and silence these denunciations, and not merely to make out a case against those who utter them,—you will at least canvass the wisdom of changing the policy on which you have entered.

THE TRUE POLICY OF THE SOUTH.

I do not say that you must abolish Slavery. That is a matter for your own people to decide. But you must permit your own people to decide it, and to discuss it freely, in order to decide it wisely. I think I know enough of sentiment at the South to be aware that it is not the largest, the wealthiest, or the most important slaveholders, who have initiated this new policy of making Slavery perpetual and paramount in their social system, and who are now pushing the attempt to its final issue. Nor is it the best minds, the most sagacious statesmen, the wisest thinkers of the South who have enlisted in it. It is rather the policy of the unthinking masses,—the great body of non-slaveholding whites, without property, without intelligence, —with nothing but the bare fact of freedom to raise them above the slave, and who see no other way of maintaining that supremacy but by perpetuating the negro Slavery on which it rests. It is this class who have nothing to lose, led on by that large class of reckless politicians who have everything to gain by ministering to the dominant passion of their society, and by excessive zeal on behalf of a system which no man is permitted to assail, who have pushed the issue to its present extreme position. It is they who have silenced freedom of speech—who frown on freedom of opinion—who trample on freedom of inquiry in regard to Slavery.

And the first and paramount duty of every Southern statesman,—every man of thought, of culture and of courage in the Southern States is, to emancipate Southern white society from this fatal thraldom. Men of this class must assert and exercise the right of canvassing the subject of Slavery fully and freely as a matter of paramount practical importance to themselves and their posterity. You know very well that there are thousands of men in the Southern States who have grave and serious doubts, to use no stronger phrase, as to the wisdom and good policy of making negro slavery the corner stone of Southern society. There are many who desire a broader foundation for the material prosperity of their section than the culture of Cotton,—and a higher moral rank among the nations than Slavery can give them. Why should they not discuss among themselves these great questions of Social and Political Economy ? Why should they be silenced in presence of the gravest questions that can engage the attention of statesmen and of States ? Would such freedom of inquiry be dangerous to the "institution ?" Then by that very fact the institution is already proved to be dangerous to the State.

But I am not prepared to believe that the peril is so imminent as to make discussion dangerous in the Southern States. On the contrary, I believe it to be the only safe guard of Southern society. It is the only condition of deliverance from the perils which hang over it. Let the strong independent minds of the South grapple with this subject as they grapple with every other. Let them look Slavery in the face,—and canvass fully and fearlessly its true relations to the welfare of Society and the growth and prosperity of the Southern States. Do you fear such a discussion ? That fear is equivalent to a surrender of the argument. Do you oppose it on the principle that Slavery is too sacred a thing to be thus canvassed and cross-examined ? It is the only institution, then, human or divine, on the face of the earth, for which you would claim such immunity. Do you say it would be playing into the hands of your enemies ? It would disarm and silence them. They would lose all motive for meddling with subjects in which they had no direct concern, when they saw them freely and conscientiously canvassed by those whose personal, social and political interests were all involved.

But such discussion you think would tend towards Emancipation. In certain sections of the South, I presume it would,—and in others, I think it would not. But even if it did, it could only be by proving that Emancipation in some form and at some time,—the prospect and the hope of ultimate Emancipation,—would promote the highest and the best interests of the Southern States. If it did not prove that,—then it would tend to fortify Slavery instead of abolishing it. My own impression is that it would show the wisdom of modifying the present system of American Slavery in certain important respects,—taking into view the substantial interests of all concerned. I think it would establish certain facts concerning the negro race which you are in danger of forgetting, and which you cannot forget or ignore with any more wisdom than a builder can forget or ignore the laws of gravity, or than an engineer can forget the explosive nature of steam. It would show that, however degraded, however ignorant, however brutal he may be, the negro has in him the seeds of humanity, and that, like all other pain and pleasure, physical and moral, like other seeds, they will inevitably grow :—that he feels men ; that he has a *will*,—a faculty of choice,—a susceptibility to motive, like any other *person*, and in spite of all laws that declare him to be merely *property* ;—that he has emotions and affections,— that he loves and hates,—that he hopes and fears,— that he yields to kindness and rebels inwardly against cruelty,—just like other men, and not at all like other " chattels." And when these facts should come to pervade the public mind, as sooner or later they must if they are facts, unless that mind is kept sealed against all access of them, they would lay the foundation for a policy on the subject of Slavery which would calm the public mind, and restore the old relations between the States and sections of the Union,—as nothing else can ever do.

There are one or two leading principles which must be recognized in the practical working of every Society, if that Society is to rest on any firm and sure foundation. One is, that every subject of Government must feel that he is under the control and guardianship of Law,—that mere caprice or whim,—the interest or the passion of another, is not the highest authority for him in any of his relations. Another is that Labor becomes valuable in proportion as it becomes intelligent. And a third is that the laborer must have something to *hope for*, as a result of his labor,—or he will never put forth the best effort of which he is capable. I am persuaded that the Southern States would find it infinitely to their advantage to incorporate these principles into their slaveholding economy. I do not believe there is a slave on any Southern plantation, who would not become more valuable by becoming more intelligent. There is not one who would not be more contented, if he could be surrounded by something of the guarantees against wrong which are essential to all society,—if he could feel that he had some place in the domestic and social economy of the world,—that his wife and children were his by law, and that no man's passion or avarice was above the law which made them so. And if every slave, thus shielded from wrong, were told that something of added good should come to him or his from increased devotion to his master's service,—

that reward should wait upon fidelity, as punishment upon evasion and crime,—that his good works should pass to the credit at least of his posterity, and that some one or more of his children should be lifted up towards freedom by his exertions on their behalf, in faithful service of their common master,—if such a system of methodized and justly modulated rewards and penalties could be interwoven with the negro slavery of the Southern States, I make no doubt that augmented peace and security would be its immediate reward and that in twenty years the whole slaveholding country would rejoice in the prospect of a degree of prosperity and power of which hitherto it has never dreamed. It is in that direction, and in that direction only, in my opinion, that safety for the slaveholding States can be found. They may tread that path however slowly,—with whatever hesitations and misgivings,—against whatever reluctancies of prejudice and pride may be inseparable from the circumstances of the case ;—the world will make allowance for all this,—and will cheer and aid the well-meant effort, however feeble and halting it may be. All the moral influences of the age,—all the motives and promptings of civilization and Christianity, all the laws of social and civil science, will be working in your behalf and no longer for your destruction. Here are problems worthy your noblest statesmen. Here are fields where the most gifted and ambitious intellects of your States may win salvation for their country and renown for themselves. How much nobler would it be for such men as you have among you, to launch out, not rashly, but with calm and courageous wisdom, upon this broad and inviting though stormy sea,—as yet untempted by the most daring prow,—than to sit down in sullen despair and hopeless inaction upon the grim and cheerless shore !

FEDERAL OBLIGATIONS OF THE SOUTH.

But again I must protest that I am speaking of things over which the Federal Government has no shadow of authority. I am only telling you what I believe to be the path of safety, of honor and of glory for the Southern States. It is for them and their statesmen to say whether they will tread it or not. Not one word have I uttered from any other motive than a profound desire for the promotion of your welfare. You will fling from you in scorn the proffered friendship—and shout execrations against us as you plunge onward, in all the reckless insolence of offended pride, into the great darkness that lies before you. You do not know the great heart of the free North, if you believe that it holds the honor and the welfare of the South in lower esteem than its own. You underrate the justice of the North, if you believe it would trample on one of your rights. You underrate its magnanimity, if you fear it would not stand by you in any extremity of danger, and wage war upon your foes as fiercely and as gladly as if they were its own. But you underrate also its courage and its power, if you expect to coerce it, by menaces or by blows, into disloyalty to the Constitution which our Fathers made, or to the fundamental principles of Liberty on which its foundations rest.

The North asks but one thing at the hands of the South,--and that is that they shall no longer cling to the Constitution of Mr. CALHOUN,—in preference to the Constitution of the United States. We ask them to abide by the principles and the policy of the Fathers of the Republic, as they read them in their speeches and their letters, and in the language and the spirit of the Constitution itself. Let us return to the sentiments, the aspirations and the hopes of WASHINGTON, and JEFFERSON, and MADISON and MASON,—Southern men and slaveholders all,—and adapt our policy and the development of our institutions, State and national, to their high and just ideals. Give us the slightest ground to hope for this,—and we will make haste to purge ourselves of all offence,—to disarm every just censure you can urge against us, and to perform, with eager and scrupulous fidelity, every constitutional and fraternal obligation that devolves upon us.

Our Government is approaching its final and decisive test. The party which represents the sentiments —just, conservative and free—of the Northern States, is soon to come into possession of the Executive power of this Republic Mr. LINCOLN, its chosen representative, becomes President of the United States on the 4th of March. You may search the country through, and you will find no more sagacious intellect, no more loyal and patriotic heart, no more sensitively and courageously just and right-meaning man than he. His whole character breathes the very spirit of our American life. His public career and his private history are alike unstained by any act, or by any word of wrong to any man or to any State. He knows no law for his public conduct but the Constitution of his country, and he recognizes no country as his but that Union, one and indivisible, which the Constitution creates. You are preparing to meet him as an enemy. You are withdrawing all the States which you and your confederates can control, into a compact and a hostile camp. Repudiating the Constitution,—repelling the supremacy of the Federal Government, —you propose to employ the intervening months before his advent in preparations to resist the constitutional authority which he will represent and wield. South Carolina has already pitched her alien tent and raised her hostile flag. Georgia, and

Alabama, and Mississippi, and possibly half a dozen more States, will imitate her example. You have an ally in the faithless and disloyal man who degrades the high place which WASHINGTON and JACKSON made equal in dignity to any throne upon the earth. Whatever may be his motive, whether he be wicked or only weak, you will have all the aid he can give you,—full impunity to perfect your plots, and all the material strength he can place within your reach. And I am quite prepared to see on the 4th of March, a solid phalanx of fifteen States,—not all, it may be, claiming to be outside the Union then, but all consenting and ready to meet the incoming Administration of Mr. LINCOLN with a peremptory demand that SLAVES SHALL BE DISTINCTLY AND UNEQUIVOCALLY RECOGNIZED AS PROPERTY BY THE CONSTITUTION OF THE UNITED STATES—as the only condition on which they will remain, or again become, members of the American Union.

And I have only to add that, in my judgment, *that demand will never be conceded.* We shall stand then, as now, upon the Constitution which our Fathers made. We shall not make a new one, nor shall we permit any human power to destroy the old one. Long before that day shall come the People of the Northern States will stand together as one man—forgetful of all past differences and party divisions—to preserve the American Union and crush any revolution which may menace it with destruction. We seek no war,—we shall wage no war except in defence of the Constitution and against its foes. But we have a country and a Constitutional Government. We know its worth to us and to mankind. and in case of necessity we are ready to tes its strength. You must not misunderstand our hopes of peace, our wish for peace,—or our readiness to make concessions for its preservation. Even if we were to concede everything you ask, we should only postpone the conflict to a later day, and throw upon our children duties and responsibilities which belong to us. I think, therefore, that the controversy should be settled now, and I have faith enough in the American people to believe that, in spite of difficulties and discouragements, by wisdom and prudent forbearance, mingled with justice and courage, on the part of their rulers, it will eventually be settled in conformity with the principles of the Constitution, and so as to promote the highest welfare of this great Republic.   I am. Sir, your obedient servant,

HENRY J. RAYMOND.